Byron

Titles in the series Critical Lives present the work of leading cultural figures of the modern period. Each book explores the life of the artist, writer, philosopher or architect in question and relates it to their major works.

In the same series

Byron

David Ellis

REAKTION BOOKS

Published by
REAKTION BOOKS LTD
Unit 32, Waterside
44–48 Wharf Road
London N1 7UX, UK
www.reaktionbooks.co.uk

First published 2023
Copyright © David Ellis 2023

All rights reserved

No part of this publication may be reproduced, stored in a retrieval system
or transmitted, in any form or by any means, electronic, mechanical,
photocopying, recording or otherwise, without the prior permission of the
publishers

Printed and bound in Great Britain by TJ Books Ltd, Padstow, Cornwall

A catalogue record for this book is available from the British Library

ISBN 978 1 78914 682 0

Contents

Prefatory Note

The events of Byron's life were so out of the ordinary, and so intimately associated with what he wrote, that it would be cheating a reader not to give some account of them. They were no doubt one of the reasons why for a long period he was regarded as a great Romantic, one of those poets who, along with Keats and Shelley, pushed through the breach in the wall of eighteenth-century literary convention first made by Wordsworth and Coleridge. Byron himself would have challenged this characterization, and, more recently, a consensus has begun to form around the idea of him as not only one of Britain's best *comic* writers, but the author, as Germaine Greer once put it, of 'the greatest comic poem in English'.[1] Supporting the first part of this claim are his letters, which are also a major source of information for his life. In the 1970s and '80s, these were excellently edited in eleven volumes by L. A. Marchand, under the title *Byron's Letters and Journals*. In order to keep my endnotes to a minimum, quotations from the letters in what follows are accompanied by an appropriate reference to Marchand's edition, prefaced by *BLJ*. For the same reason, all quotations from Byron's poems are followed in my text by references to either the seven volumes of Byron's *Complete Poetical Works* (*CPW*), compiled and edited by Jerome J. McGann, or, where it is possible to cite an alternative – given the cost of those volumes – to McGann's *Lord Byron: The Major Works* (*LB*), in the Oxford World's Classics series (2008), where the same texts are used.

Thomas Phillips, *Byron*, 1813, oil on canvas.

1

Early Days

Towards the end of 1815, after barely a year of marriage, Byron exhibited so many peculiarities of behaviour that his wife became convinced he must be mad. There were details in his family background that might have led a superficial observer to endorse the same view. His mother was Catherine Gordon, a Scot from a family that could trace its lineage back to the Stuarts. They were the proprietors of Gight Castle and a large estate northwest of Aberdeen, and it was at Gight that Catherine's paternal grandfather drowned in circumstances which strongly suggested suicide. When in 1779 her father met a near-identical fate, it was not in Scotland but in Bath, where he had brought Catherine. Suicide is often assumed to take place when the balance of the mind is disturbed, but it can also be described as a consequence of deep depression, a feeling (which Byron often had) that the world, and our relation to it, is such as not to make life worth living.

Scottish inheritance laws being more favourable to women than those in England, Catherine became the thirteenth 'laird of Gight' on the death of her father and worth around £23,000. This made her, on the contemporary marriage market and in the unpleasant jargon of the day, 'a golden Dolly': someone with the resources to rescue an impoverished male member of the upper classes from his debts. It was when she was back in Bath at the age of 21 that Catherine attracted the attention of 'mad Jack Byron', as he had

Thomas Stewardson (1781–1859), *Mrs Catherine Gordon Byron, 1765–1811*, oil on canvas.

become known, not it would seem because he was a lunatic but on account of wildly unconventional, devil-may-care behaviour. A former captain in the Coldstream Guards, and the eldest son of a vice admiral, 'mad Jack' had caused a major scandal by running off with the wife of the Marquess of Carmarthen. Obtaining a divorce was extremely difficult in the late eighteenth century, but a little less so if you happened to be a peer. In 1779, after the House of Lords had granted Lady Carmarthen's husband a divorce, she and Jack married and went to live mostly in France in what must have been some style given that the divorce proceedings had not deprived her of an annual income of £4,000. French living can have been no hardship for Jack, who had spent part of his youth in a military academy in France and who was often to be found in that country subsequently, although chiefly because that was where he felt safe from being arrested for debt. This eventuality became increasingly likely after 1784, because in that year his wife died and her income disappeared with her. The only surviving child from this first marriage was Augusta, who was thus the half-sister of the Lord Byron who is the subject of this book and would play an important role in his life.

When mad Jack Byron turned up in Bath in 1785 his debts were already huge and crippling. A relatively naive young girl with a Scottish accent may have had other attractions for a handsome, sophisticated rake such as he was, but all the evidence suggests that the chief one was her £23,000. For a man who had been living on £4,000 a year this was not huge, but it was preferable to a debtors' prison. After the marriage ceremony, the couple spent some time in the castle at Gight and then were to be found in a bewildering number of locations, in both England and France, chiefly because the liquidation of Catherine's assets was a slow process and Jack's creditors were forever on his tail. It was during this period that Catherine nursed her stepdaughter Augusta through a childhood illness, a service which does not seem to have softened the girl's subsequent dislike of her father's second wife.

By 1787, Catherine was pregnant with her first, and what would be her only, child. A reasonably fashionable lodging for her lying-in was secured in London, but on 22 January 1788 Jack was absent for the birth of his son, George Gordon Byron, as he was christened, perhaps because he was again hiding from his creditors. After Catherine had taken her baby back up to Aberdeen in what was probably the following year, Jack joined his family there for a short period. With the castle no longer available, they lived in rented lodgings in the town, but it was not long before he found his wife's company intolerable and took a separate rental at the other end of the same street. The explosive temper Catherine was later to manifest may have already begun to show itself, which would not be surprising given the exploitation she had suffered; but the couple's very different backgrounds made them ill-matched in any case. In September 1790 Jack left Aberdeen and went to stay with his sister in Valenciennes. Because this town in northern France was where he died in August of the following year, Catherine never saw him again. She was apparently heartbroken at the news of his death, having always entertained towards him something of the same ambivalent feelings she would show in her relations with her son, admiring and loving this handsome ne'er-do-well while at the same time deeply resenting his failings.

Mad Jack's son may not have been insane, as his wife would later believe, but there were occasions when his behaviour went well beyond what would usually be regarded as normal. Some biographers have found explanations for this not so much in his genetic inheritance as his upbringing (in nurture not nature). An early poem called 'Childish Recollections' describes how being sent to an English public school led to his forming friendships that compensated for 'the love denied at home'. 'Stern Death', he goes on to explain,

> forbade my orphan youth to share,
> The tender guidance of a Father's care;
> Can Rank, or ev'n a Guardian's name supply,
> The Love, which glistens in a Father's eye? (*CPW* I.165)

Passing moral judgements on individuals who died many years ago is a hazardous business, but it is doubtful whether Jack Byron's eye often glistened with love for his son George, or indeed for his daughter Augusta. She was shuttled between various rich relatives, one of these being the 'Guardian' Byron mentions in the lines above. This was the Earl of Carlisle, who was the son of mad Jack's aunt and took on that role when, on the death of a great-uncle, the ten-year-old Byron moved to England with his mother and became a lord.

For Byron to talk of 'the love denied at home' would seem an obvious criticism of his mother, and it is true his relationship with her was often stormy with, as he points out somewhat mawkishly in 'Childish Recollections', no siblings in the vicinity to share the family tensions: 'What Brother springs a Brother's love to seek/ What sister's gentle kiss has prest my cheek?' Her hot temper was the subject of an epitaph her young son wrote for her long before she was dead: 'Such were her vocal powers, her temper such,/ That all who knew them both exclaimed "Too much!"' (*CPW* I.11). All the signs suggest that the problem between mother and son was compounded by Byron having a fiery temper much like her own, while her most frequent complaint about her son, especially as he moved into adolescence, was that he was 'just like his father'. This could have meant, and perhaps sometimes did mean, that her son was becoming equally seductive and good-looking; but its chief sense was clearly that he was in danger of being just as selfish and irresponsible. Treated as she had been by mad Jack, it was perhaps inevitable that she should sometimes have not only tried to ensure that he did not become like his dead father, but been inclined to make her son suffer in his stead.

The other reproach Byron reports his mother making is less easy to explain or excuse since he records that in one of her 'fits of passion' she had called him 'a lame brat'.[1] This was a reference to his having been born with a deformed right foot. There is still some debate about whether this should be described as 'clubbed', but it appears to have been turned in at the ankle so that the young boy had to walk on its side and wear specially made boots. A further consequence was that the right leg ended up shorter than the other, with the result that there could hardly ever have been a time when Byron did not limp. In her exasperation with her son's behaviour, Mrs Byron may well have reminded him that he was lame, but at least she could not be accused of ignoring his disability, since she spent a lot of time, as well as a good deal of money she could hardly afford, trying to find medical treatment to cure the problem. Not surprisingly, these treatments brought the young boy a great deal of pain and discomfort, but had little or no permanent effect.

Not everyone noticed that Byron limped, and he became practised in avoiding situations where it would become noticeable. Nor was his disability so severe as to stop him participating in many of the usual boyhood sports. He was proud, for example, of having taken part in a cricket match between Harrow and Eton, and when he was an undergraduate and young man about town, he hired the best boxing and fencing coaches, both of which activities require a degree of nimble footwork. But the exercise he appears to have enjoyed most was nevertheless one where any physical disadvantage for which he had to compensate was minimal. Everyone who read *Don Juan* would later learn that in May 1810 he had equalled the feat of Leander by swimming the Hellespont, the stretch of water now known as the Dardanelles, but even before that he had swum much longer distances, in London's Thames and the Tagus in Portugal, and when he was living in Venice he describes a swimming competition which involved being in the water for over four hours. That the men on his mother's side of the family appear to have had a predisposition for drowning themselves did not lessen his addiction to swimming from a very early age.

In regretting the early loss of his father, whom he can barely have known or remembered, Byron is also indicating that he was starved of affection as a child. This is a difficult claim to evaluate yet there are episodes in Byron's early life which do suggest someone with an

W. Walker and W. Angus after Paul Sandby, *Newstead Priory, Nottinghamshire*, 1779, etching and engraving.

abnormal craving for more love than he felt he had ever received. The first of these involved a young Scottish cousin called Mary Duff, whom he came to see a lot of while he was still in Aberdeenshire. He later described having fallen desperately in love with this girl when he was only eight years old and at a time when, he explicitly claims, his feelings were without any sexual element. Much later, when he was an adolescent, there was another Mary, Mary Chaworth, to whom he became hopelessly attached. The Chaworths were an old family from the English gentry whose estates bordered those of Newstead Abbey, where the Byrons were established. By the time Byron fell in love with her he was at public school and his mother, in expectation that he would go from there to university and would therefore not need Newstead for a while, had rented the whole estate out to a young aristocrat called Lord Grey de Ruthyn and taken for herself a house in the charming town of Southwell, about 30 kilometres (20 mi.) away. But Lord Grey clearly liked Byron and invited him to stay at Newstead whenever he wanted, so he was able to see a good deal of Mary. The trouble was that he was only fifteen, whereas Mary was three years older and already had her eye on a more suitable future partner among the local gentry. Since many of the poems Byron was to write about her implied a feeling of betrayal, and he was so patently infatuated, she may have flirted with him a little but, according to Byron himself, the relationship came to an abrupt end when he either overheard Mary saying to her maid, or had reported to him, 'Do you think I could care any thing for that lame boy?'[2] While he still had hopes of earning her love, the strength of his feeling can be gauged by the fact that he resisted all his mother's pleas that he should go back to school and ended up missing a whole term.

That George Gordon Byron became a lord more or less by accident strengthened the fatalism that was one of the features of

The house in Southwell that Byron's mother rented (today).

his character, and may have had something to do with the Calvinist doctrines of his early teachers. His grandfather was after all only a younger brother of the Lord Byron from whom he inherited the title and whose most direct male descendant was, by the 1790s, a grandson. But this young man was killed by a stray shot at the siege of the Corsican city of Calvi in 1794. Catherine Gordon had become a 'laird' when she was fifteen, but from the age of six Byron knew that he was destined to be a peer. Or at least his mother did. The full reality probably first came home in 1798, after news of his predecessor's death reached Aberdeen, and he was invited by a teacher at his grammar school to share some cake and wine in celebration of his new status. This pedagogically dubious move must have immediately made clear to the boy that lords tend to be treated differently from other people, and begun a process of acute social self-consciousness, the outcomes of which were to prompt many biographers, beginning with Tom Moore, to suggest that Byron was a snob. Certainly, some of his early poems reveal a preoccupation with lineage, and an aspect of his unusually intense youthful ambition is a determination to be worthy of the ancestors he believed had distinguished themselves in the Crusades, or during the English Civil War, and could trace their origins back to the Norman Conquest.

The Newstead Abbey which Byron and his mother took over in 1798 was in a dilapidated state but it represented a huge change from rented lodgings in Aberdeen. All that Catherine Gordon had been able to rescue from her £23,000 was an annuity of £150, so she was aware that she could not afford the education appropriate to her son's new status. With the help of John Hanson, the man who became the family lawyer, she therefore approached the Earl of Carlisle, the most powerful as well as the richest of Byron's English relatives. In agreeing to become the boy's guardian, the earl also secured for him from the government £500 a year to pay for his education up to the age of 21, as well as some extra money for

Catherine. In the economic distress that followed the ending of the Napoleonic Wars, when taxes had to be raised to service what had become a huge national debt, a good deal of justifiable criticism would be directed at this way the English aristocracy had of looking after its own.

After some tutoring in Nottingham, Byron was sent to a prep school in Dulwich before going on to Harrow in April 1801. At the beginning, he was not at all happy there. As someone who limped and had a Scottish accent, he might well have been a candidate for bullying were it not that he was notably pugnacious, always ready to use his fists in either his own defence or that of anyone he felt was similarly vulnerable. The difficulty appeared rather that he was slow to make friends, but when he looked back on his Harrow schooldays in 'Childish Recollections', it was to see himself partly as the leader of a gang which participated in exhilarating scuffles with the locals ('I like a row, & always did from a boy,' he was later to tell Walter Scott; *BLJ* IX.86). But he also reflected nostalgically on the very warm friendships, the romantic attachments it would be more accurate to say, he had eventually made at Harrow. Some of these were with boys his own age but others with younger ones whom the school's 'fagging' system, in which the junior boys were made to act as the servants of their seniors, temporarily put under his control. This could have done little to discourage that idealized version of what were essentially pederastic relationships which the boys could garner from some of the authors who were at the core of their training in the classics. How confirmed Byron was in his inclination to become attached to boys slightly younger than himself became evident when he moved on from Harrow to Trinity College, Cambridge, in October 1805 and fell deeply in love with a chorister called John Edleston.

The obvious question to ask is just how physical these relations to other boys or men became; but it is very difficult to answer. Even though the number of executions each year remained very low (unlike those for theft), sodomy was a capital offence in Byron's day; but he talks fairly openly about his love for others of his own sex in his poetry, and in his letters. It seems improbable he would have done this had the relationships not been acceptably platonic, and therefore it is unlikely that he had any experience of their full physical aspects until he was on his grand tour of the Ottoman Empire between 1809 and 1811, and living in countries where they were more easily accepted. Yet he was a daring individual, always ready to follow his instincts rather than submit to convention, and what happened in private between the men and boys he loved we can never know. The usual assumption has been that Byron was certainly bisexual, but one fairly recent biographer has organized the story of his life around the idea that his nature was fundamentally homosexual and that all of his many heterosexual affairs were substitutes or compensations for instincts the law of his own country obliged him to suppress.[3] If that was so, all one can say is that Byron did a remarkable amount of compensating.

Greek and above all Latin were at the centre of his education at Harrow and, for all his intense ambition to make his mark, Byron was not especially distinguished in either. A former Harrovian who has studied his time at the school has concluded that he achieved little in the academic line and that, if he shone at all, it was in 'making trouble, public speaking and passionate friendships'.[4] Looking at what was on offer in both the English public schools and the universities, Thomas Moore felt that the syllabuses might have been explicitly designed to prevent gifted individuals from becoming poets; but he was able to consult a memorandum book of Byron's in which he noted an impressively long list of all the books he had read in his youth.[5] This shows how voracious a reader he must have been at that time, but chiefly in history and literature. Like Wordsworth when he was at Cambridge, Byron seems to have followed only what most absorbed him while paying scant attention to the official syllabus.

Two exercises Byron clearly did find interesting at Harrow, however, were translating Latin verse into an English equivalent and the public speaking that the historian of Harrow mentions. The latter refers to preparation for an annual 'speech day', when, in contrast to today, when pupils are usually lectured to, it was they themselves who declaimed in front of the whole school and invited guests. The exercise was no doubt meant to accustom them to a future life in politics, given that some would, like Byron, automatically become members of Parliament (one of those at school with Byron was Robert Peel). Preparing for these events excited him and he did well in them, choosing King Lear's address to the storm as his contribution on the last occasion he performed. It seems strange at first that a youth whose disability had, in so many other respects, made him acutely self-conscious and shy should have enjoyed performing in this way, but it was one of the many paradoxes of his character that he was also 'theatrical'. This was evident in his fondness, throughout his life, for dressing up: in the special robes his rank entitled him to wear in Cambridge, for example, the Eastern costumes he bought while on his grand tour or the uniforms he had specially made when he decided to join the struggle for Greek independence.

Once he accepted that he was making no headway with Mary Chaworth, and after a mysterious incident in which he may have indignantly rejected some kind of sexual overture from Lord Grey, Byron no longer visited Newstead and made do with Southwell, in spite of his stormy relations with his mother. Between 1804 and 1807, that is, his later teenage years, Byron was increasingly to be found there, mainly because, shy though he was with new acquaintances, he had managed to make such lively and interesting friends in the town. Chief among these were John and Elizabeth Pigot, the children of a doctor's widow who lived in a house more or less opposite his mother's. They introduced him to the sons and daughters of several other upper-class families in the area, and it

Page from Elizabeth Pigot's booklet showing Byron in the bath and his dog worrying a cat.

was in what must have been the sufficiently large drawing room of one of these that it was decided to put on a couple of plays, not once but on three successive nights. Since the plays were very different (Richard Cumberland's *The Wheel of Fortune* and a two-act farce by John Allingham called *The Weathercock*), Byron showed his versatility by playing the principal parts in both.

It was in the sympathetic atmosphere of Southwell that Byron first became not only an amateur actor but a writer, or at least felt free to indulge a facility for writing verse of which he was already aware. He got on particularly well with Elizabeth, who was in her early twenties, and something of the nature of their relationship, and how ready she was to tease him, can be gauged by a booklet she both wrote and illustrated detailing *The Wonderful History of Lord Byron and His Dog*. Written in a doggerel that the pair clearly often exchanged, this booklet focused on two aspects of Byron's behaviour or character that are worth mentioning. One was his extreme fondness for animals, particularly dogs. He had with him in Southwell a large Newfoundland dog called Bosen, or Boatswain, to whom he was especially attached. When he went up to Cambridge at the end of 1805, he wanted to take a dog with him – it was then probably in retaliation to the authorities' refusal to allow him to do so that he somehow acquired a bear, which he would occasionally lead through the Cambridge streets. After Bosen died in 1808, Byron famously had a monument erected to him in the courtyard at Newstead and had carved on it an epitaph, which concludes: 'To mark a friend's remains these stones arise,/ I never had but one, and here he lies' (*cpw* I.225). Byron was interested in all kinds of animals, in addition to dogs, and would have made a good zookeeper had he not been a poet.

Elizabeth Pigot's booklet is chiefly concerned with the trouble Byron's dog caused him: 'He went into the house & sat down to writing,' she says, 'And when he had done, Found Bosen was fighting.' Again: 'He went into the Bath, to boil off his Fat,/ And when he was there, Bos'en worried the Cat.' This last episode, amusingly illustrated with Byron in a hip bath, is the second aspect of which the booklet is a reminder. It seems to have been at Southwell above all that Byron realized he was following in his portly mother's footsteps and putting on weight ('a fat bashful boy' is how Elizabeth describes him on their first meeting[6]). He decided to do something about this and, with a characteristic exertion of willpower, began a regime of vigorous exercise, including the use

Tomb of Byron's dog Boatswain, in the courtyard of Newstead Abbey.

of hot baths (one of which Elizabeth is describing), together with a draconian if somewhat eccentric regime of dieting: for many years there were periods when his main meal seems to have been a dish of potatoes flavoured with vinegar. Around 5' 8", he weighed over 90 kilograms (14 st.) when he first went to university but was under 70 by the time he left. Writing to Elizabeth from Cambridge in June 1807, having spent much of the preceding year in Southwell (regular attendance at educational institutions not being his strong point), he reported that he had already so changed his shape that some people no longer recognized him.

What is remarkable about his friendship with Elizabeth is how open he felt he could be with her. In a letter from Cambridge written in July 1807 he responds to what must have been her request to tell her more about his 'protégé', saying that John Edleston had been his '*almost constant* associate' since he first arrived in Trinity College and that 'I certainly *love* him more than any human being.'

Their possible plan after university, he goes on, was to live together, in which case,

> We shall put *Lady E. Butler, & Miss Ponsonby* to the
> *Blush*, *Pylades & Orestes* out of countenance, & want
> nothing but a *Catastrophe* like *Ninus & Euryalus*, to
> give *Jonathan & David* the 'go by'. (*BLJ* I.125)

The two ladies he mentions were famous or notorious for living together as a married couple, and Byron's other references indicate how classical, and indeed biblical, precedents could be invoked to sanction close male friendships. But what seems unlikely is that he would write to Elizabeth Pigot in this way if he were actually sleeping with Edleston, unusually broad-minded though she clearly was. It appears rather that close male friendship could be talked about in this period without sexual intimacy being automatically assumed.

2
First Publications

According to Byron, it was the sympathetic group of friends he found in Southwell who suggested he should publish a collection of the poems that he was in the process of writing or had already written, if only privately. This was the declared origin of *Fugitive Pieces* (November 1806), which was printed in the nearby town of Newark and meant principally for them. Not all these friends were young, and he formed a strong bond with a relation of the Pigots called John Becher, who was almost twenty years older than Byron and the vicar of a local parish. He seems to have functioned as a substitute father figure for the still very young Byron, who took his advice seriously – seriously enough in this instance to have the hundred or so copies of *Fugitive Pieces* withdrawn and destroyed and then have printed almost immediately another edition, titled *Poems on Various Occasions*. A number of alterations were made to this new edition to ensure that his Southwell friends would not be shocked, including the removal of a poem that Becher felt ought never to have been published.

The poem in question was called 'To Mary' and is almost certainly not concerned with the Mary whose second name was Chaworth since it strongly implies she either had sex with Byron or came very close, but then drove him into 'jealous rage' by transferring her favours to someone else. He describes himself as smiling 'to think how oft we've done,/ What prudes declare a sin to act is' and, looking back, decides ''tis most delight/ To view each other panting, dying,/ In love's *extatic posture* lying'. If the gods

HOURS OF IDLENESS,

A

SERIES OF POEMS,

ORIGINAL

AND

TRANSLATED,

By GEORGE GORDON, LORD BYRON,

A MINOR.

Μητ' αρ με μαλ' αινει μητι τι νεικει.
HOMER. Iliad, 10.

Virginibus puerisque Canto.
HORACE.

He whistled as he went for want of thought.
DRYDEN.

Newark:

Printed and sold by S. and J. RIDGE;

SOLD ALSO BY B. CROSBY AND CO. STATIONER'S COURT;
LONGMAN, HURST, REES, AND ORME, PATERNOSTER-
ROW; F. AND C. RIVINGTON, ST. PAUL'S CHURCH-
YARD; AND J. MAWMAN, IN THE POULTRY,
LONDON.

1807.

Title page of *Hours of Idleness* (1807).

could have seen what he was up to with Mary, he concludes, they would have never 'fancied us offending,/ But *wisely* followed our *example*' (*CPW* I.134–5). 'To Mary' was the first recorded instance of Byron's encounters with what he was later to denounce as cant. He suppressed the poem reluctantly and later, in a number of satirical poems directed at what he felt was the prudery and hypocrisy of his Southwell critics, expressed his resentment at having had to do so, explaining at the same time that 'When Love's delirium haunts the glowing mind,/ Limping Decorum lingers far behind' (*CPW* I.180). Yet he continued to correspond with Becher and must have known he had overstepped the mark.

The reception of what had been *Fugitive Pieces* and became *Poems on Various Occasions* was nevertheless sufficiently favourable to make Byron feel it was worth approaching a wider public, especially as he was now writing so many new poems. It was this feeling that helped give rise to *Hours of Idleness*, his first publication addressed to the public at large. As a writer still in his teens, Byron is almost inevitably highly derivative, and a chief model for those poems which deal with love is the work of Thomas Moore, who would become Byron's close friend as well as his biographer. In his early work (published under the name Thomas Little) Moore had acquired a reputation for being dangerously erotic, but this was offset by the advantage he had of being able to sing well, so he could find settings for the poems he wrote and then perform them with great success in London drawing rooms. Byron was no singer, but from the beginning of his writing career many of his short lyrics have an engaging rhythm and simplicity appropriate for musical setting, as Beethoven was later to demonstrate with several of them.

Love poems involving putative partners who were either men or women, translations of the classics and echoes of the new Romanticism, mainly in its Scottish, 'Ossianic' form, are accompanied in these early poems by playful, satirical pieces foregrounding Byron's strong sense of humour. Anyone interested

William Finden, after Sir Thomas Lawrence, *Thomas Moore*, 1836, stipple and line engraving.

enough to read through them at the time might well have wondered in which direction Byron's talent would eventually take him, although they ought to have been convinced that, despite all their sentimentality and clichéd language, it would be certain to take him somewhere worthwhile. His first reviews were in fact broadly favourable, and Byron also secured some endorsements, including one from Henry Mackenzie, the Scottish author of *The Man of Feeling*, a novel which had made a considerable stir when it was first published in 1771 and is still sometimes read today. To be approved of by Mackenzie was no small achievement, but, as far as Edinburgh was concerned, the endorsement Byron really craved was from its already celebrated *Review*. He looked forward to what its famously severe contributors would make of his work with a good deal of trepidation, the same kind of anxiety evident in an ill-judged introductory note or preface which he decided to attach to *Hours of Idleness*.

Byron pointed out in this prefatory note that he was still only nineteen and had written many of the poems when he was two or three years younger. To this quasi-apology he added several reminders that he was a peer who, in the future, was likely to have better things to do than trouble the public a second time with what were after all only the fruits of 'lighter hours' (*CPW* I.32–4). These disclaimers were in spite of the fact that, with his keen desire to succeed, he had as yet no clear idea of how to employ the hours which were not light. Life at Cambridge was teaching him that he had neither the talent nor the inclination to become a famous scholar or intellectual, and he seems already to have been ruling out the army. Writing to one of the close friends he had made in Harrow, who, by 1807, had joined mad Jack's old regiment, the Coldstream Guards, he insisted that he could not conquer his resistance to 'a Life absolutely & exclusively devoted to Carnage' (*BLJ* I.118). His view here may have been influenced by the fact that this was the period of the Napoleonic Wars and, when Byron was at

Harrow, he had persisted in harbouring by his bed a small statue of Napoleon, whom at that time he admired. Another path to glory for someone of his rank would be politics, but, like his mother, Byron was a Whig and it was the Tories who were massively dominant while Britain was at war.

His real abilities lay in writing, but his preface to *Hours of Idleness* shows him haunted by the idea, which he never quite abandoned, that this activity was somehow *infra dig* for a person of his rank (for a long time he refused to take any money for his writings). 'Poetry, however,' he wrote, 'is not my primary vocation; to divert the dull moments of indisposition, or the monotony of a vacant hour' urged him 'to this sin'. For people who took poetry seriously and were not lords, these methods, which a nervous young author utilized in order to placate what, he worried, might be a hostile response, were like red rags to a bull, although the hostility of the anonymous reviewer (who was not the *Edinburgh Review*'s chief editor, Francis Jeffrey, as Byron long thought, but Henry Brougham) proved extreme enough to make one feel that he already knew something about Byron which he did not like. Brougham claimed that there was nothing in *Hours of Idleness* which rose above a dead flat, so the whole collection was like a pool of stagnant water. Youth was no excuse, in that there were many young people who could write just as poorly but did not, the implication is, publish their works. Brougham quotes passages that are certainly mediocre, and as for those imitations in Byron's volume of the immensely popular 'Ossian' – the legendary Gaelic bard from the second or third century AD whose epic poetry was offered to the public from 1760 onwards by James Macpherson in what he falsely implied was more or less direct translation – Brougham claims not to be able to make head or tail of them but accepts they 'look very like Macpherson' in that 'they are pretty nearly as stupid and tiresome.' He accuses Byron of egotism, which is true enough in the sense that his verse was from the start both autobiographical and self-revealing, and, noting that this peer has said '"it is highly improbable from his situation and pursuits hereafter" that he should again condescend to become an author,' he concludes by suggesting that readers ought to be thankful for this assurance and not 'look the gift horse in the mouth'.[1]

Given that these remarks were made in the country's most influential organ of literary opinion, and about an author just starting out, they ought to have been devastating for Byron, and to some extent they were. Someone who was less naturally and compulsively a writer, or less instinctively combative, might well have taken the hint and given up. Additionally wounding was that, in a period when literary judgement was very closely tied to political affiliation, the comments were to be found in a Whig journal. At Cambridge Byron had joined a new Whig club which a fellow undergraduate, John Cam Hobhouse, had recently launched. For a while, the way his poems had been treated in the *Edinburgh Review* made him think of resigning, but better thoughts soon prevailed.

Hobhouse was not the only new friend Byron had made after he dragged himself away from Southwell theatricals, and poetry publication, and returned to Cambridge in the summer and autumn of 1807. Moore was later to claim that if most of Byron's close friends were not aristocrats it was because his pride inclined him to choose from a rank lower than his own; but that is a charge hardly borne out by the facts. Hobhouse was from a rich but dissenting family rather than the Anglican establishment, but he had attended Westminster School and proved he was no intellectual slouch by winning one of Trinity's college prizes. Scrope Davies, who had been a pupil at Eton and around this time also became one of Byron's intimates, was clever enough to become a fellow of King's College, Cambridge; while Charles Matthews, also an Etonian and particularly admired by Byron for his intelligence, had competed for and easily won the first elected fellowship offered

W. J. Newton (1785–1869), *John Cam Hobhouse*, miniature on ivory.

by the recently founded Downing College (the examination papers
still exist). As this suggests, and as their correspondence with Byron
shows, they were all clever men not inclined to defer to Byron just
because he was a lord, and his warm friendship with all three had
little to do with rank. If he was closest to Hobhouse, with whom
the bond was lifelong, it was perhaps because he also wrote verse

and in 1809 would publish a collection which included some short poems by Byron (and one or two by other members of Trinity College), but was mostly his own work. A fourth friend from this period was also an author, as well as a translator, like Hobhouse, of Juvenal. But Francis Hodgson, although another fellow of King's College, falls into a slightly different category, since he was seven years older than Byron, had been his tutor and must already have been thinking of becoming a clergyman.

The longest poems in Hobhouse's collection were 'imitations' of satires by not only Juvenal but Horace. Byron had already shown a talent for this kind of verse and, partly in conjunction with Hobhouse, had been spending some time writing a satire on 'the poetry of the present day'. It was this which, after he had digested the criticisms of the *Edinburgh Review,* was then transformed into *English Bards and Scotch Reviewers.* With the help of a distant relation called Robert Dallas, who had appeared out of the woodwork, and was a clergyman with a number of 'improving' books to his name, this spirited response was published anonymously just over a year after Brougham's review had appeared. Since it was a success, Byron very quickly produced a second edition in which he added around three hundred more lines, as well as a preface in prose, and made it clear that he was the author. This was completed only months before he sailed off to Lisbon, in July 1809, to begin a grand tour of the East.

There were times in Byron's life when his style of living was unusually, not to say frantically, dissipated and the period between leaving Cambridge in December 1807 and setting out on his grand tour in June 1809 was one of them. Alongside the new friends he had made at university, he was often in London or Brighton and claimed at one point that he was keeping at least two mistresses. The letter that Byron wrote to Elizabeth Pigot about Edleston was frank, but even franker was the one he dispatched to Belcher, the *Reverend* John Belcher, on 20 February 1808. He said then that he had just had a prescription from a doctor 'not for any *complaint* but for *debility*, and literally *too much Love*'. His 'blue eyed Caroline', he explained, 'who is only sixteen, has been lately so *charming*, that though we are both in perfect health, we are at present commanded to *repose*, being nearly worn out'. The tone of his letter to Belcher is hardly different from that in the one he wrote to Hobhouse on the following day, where he described himself as 'buried in an abyss of sensuality', and then added that, though he has 'renounced *hazard*' (a game played with dice for money), he is 'given to Harlots' (*BLJ* 1.157–8).

There is in one of Byron's letters an interesting defence of gambling as the one vice of which you can never tire – that he gave it up makes one wonder how he came to accumulate debts of over £20,000 before he left England. His £500 a year being nowhere near enough, he had raised money on the expectation of the assets he would presumably control when he reached 21. To do this he needed a guarantor and, realizing that of course he could not ask his mother to fulfil this function, and having tentatively approached John Hansen, he turned at one point to his half-sister, Augusta. While he was still at Harrow he had begun to establish with her, through a series of letters, the kind of warm and affectionate bond his nature clearly needed, particularly valuing the fact that she was someone to whom he could be as critical as he liked about his mother. But when Augusta realized the financial difficulties in which he wanted to involve her, she became alarmed and revealed what was going on to other members of the family. This led to a cooling off in her relationship with him which was only properly re-established after his return from abroad. Not that Augusta's behaviour made much difference, since Byron quickly found others to help him raise quick money at exorbitant interest. Some of this may have gone on gambling, but most appears to have been spent on carriages, horses, servants, prostitutes, boxing and fencing lessons, and a host of other items that were required for a young aristocrat living the high life. Part of the problem seems also to have been that Byron was acutely conscious of what was expected of a young lord with prospects like his (*noblesse oblige*). Shortly before he left the country, a friend with whom he had no doubt frequented the London clubs was killed in a duel, leaving his wife and children without resources. When Byron went to visit the widow, he left behind a note for £500 (not, of course, from his own store of money but from the sums he had borrowed).

When Byron left Cambridge, it was with an ill-deserved master's degree, since he had not even fulfilled the only serious requirement for a lord, which was to have 'resided' for a set number of terms; but allowances were made. One way of alleviating his financial problem would have been to dispose of an estate in Rochdale, Lancashire, which the Byrons still owned (his official title was in fact Baron Rochdale), but his predecessor's illegal sale of its mining rights involved difficulties which made it hard to move forward on that front quickly. The solution would have been selling Newstead, but at this stage Byron was resolved not to do this ('I will at least transmit it to the next lord'; *BLJ* I.175). Remarkably enough given her own past history, his mother felt the only solution was for her son to marry some rich heiress. She believed he had a good chance of doing so because he was not just a member of the upper classes, as her own husband had been, but a peer. The idea was obviously also in Byron's own head because in December 1808 he wrote to Hanson, 'I suppose it will end in my marrying a *Golden Dolly* or blowing my brains out, it does not much matter which, the Remedies are nearly alike' (*CPW* I.181).

Lord Grey's lease on Newstead had expired in June 1808 and Byron returned to live there for a while, keeping his mother at bay in Southwell by explaining that he was busy having suitable accommodation arranged and redecorated for her so that she could live comfortably in the Abbey while he was away in the East. Friends were invited down and Matthews later wrote an informative letter describing one of Byron's house parties. No one seemed to get up before midday; the afternoons were spent reading, walking, riding, playing sports or practising pistol shooting in the former cloisters of the renovated medieval building; and there was an abundance of food and drink, including 'the finest wines of France', some of which were drunk from a human skull that Byron had had fashioned into a drinking goblet. This was a 'Gothic' touch which went well with the monks' costumes Byron also provided for his guests. 'The evening diversions may be easily conceived,' Matthews rather disappointingly comments (he is writing to a woman), but it is likely they included female company, although that would have been of no interest to him since, from the way his friends wrote and referred to him, it would appear he was interested in young boys rather than young girls.[2] How these latter might have been supplied so far away from London as Nottingham is not evident, but Byron did not confine his sexual activities to known centres of vice like the capital or Brighton. His poems and letters reveal that by the time he left England he was already the father of two children, the mother of at least one of these being a servant at Newstead. We know he settled an annuity of £100 on her and the child ('I cannot have the girl on the parish'), but there are no surviving details of what happened in the other case (*BLJ* I.189 and 210).

Struggling with his debts and preparing to go away, Byron was also continuing to work hard on *English Bards and Scotch Reviewers*. The case for believing that Bryon's most lasting contribution to English literature is not so much in lyric or narrative poetry, and nor in the drama, but as a comic writer both in verse and in his letters is strong. *English Bards and Scotch Reviewers* is his first extended offering in satire, and a remarkable achievement for a very young man, yet by 1816 he had come to regret that it had ever been written because some parts of it were, he said, too 'personal' and the overall tone less genial than, by that date, he had come to believe it ought to have been. In his prose preface he claims that his aim was 'not to prove that I can write well, but, *if possible*, to make others write better' (*cpw* I.228). Yet, in the work which follows, any reforming mission there might have been takes a distant second place to demonstrating, for the benefit of the Edinburgh reviewers in particular, how widely read he was in modern literature and how sharp and witty he could be. In lines he added to the beginning of his poem, he referred to himself as having been, in his previous incarnation as an author, 'A school-boy freak, unworthy praise or blame' (*lb* 3), and set out to show that there was far more to him than that.

What is remarkable is that Byron is prepared to take on almost the whole of the current literary establishment, beginning with Walter Scott, whom he urges to devote his undoubted genius to topics rather more elevated than 'the vile fury of a plundering clan,/ Whose proudest deeds disgrace the name of man' (*cpw* I.258). It was after his return from the East that Byron got to know Scott and became very friendly with him (that they were both lame was a factor in drawing them together). Several other of the figures he mocks in *English Bards and Scotch Reviewers* also became his friends, which may have been one of the reasons why, when a fifth edition of the poem was being prepared, he decided to suppress it. From attacking Scott, Byron goes on to tackle Wordsworth and Coleridge, calling the former someone 'Who, both by precept and example, shows/ That prose is verse, and verse is merely prose,' and suggesting that anyone who reads 'The Idiot Boy' is likely to 'Conceive the Bard the hero of the story' (*cpw* I.236). These passages, like those which accuse Coleridge of obscurity, may well be the best known in *English Bards and Scotch Reviewers*, probably because the work of their targets is still read. (The problem with satirical verse, as Pope's *Dunciad* illustrates, is that it tends to become less interesting the more its victims sink into obscurity.) Byron was later to be convinced by Shelley that there was far more to Wordsworth than his supposed preoccupation with idiots, and in getting to know Coleridge personally he came to admire him. But the third 'lake poet' Byron attacks is Robert Southey (accused of the over-production of boring verse epics), with whom his relations only worsened over time.

With the next poet on his hit list, however, an especially warm and intimate bond would grow. The criticism Byron directs at Thomas Moore shows him nonchalantly prepared to mock fellow writers for features he had already demonstrated in his own verse. It was under the influence of Moore that he wrote those poems or stanzas in *Fugitive Pieces* which so shocked some of his Southwell acquaintances, but now he makes fun of him as the 'young Catullus of his day,/ As sweet, but as immoral in his lay', classifying Moore among the 'melodious advocates of lust' (*CPW* I.237–8). But the references are playful and mainly useful in allowing him to focus his attention on Jeffrey as the presumed reviewer of *Hours of Idleness*, and whom he first of all imagines in terms of an entirely bogus relationship to Judge Jeffries (who was Welsh, not Scottish), the notorious 'hanging judge' of the seventeenth century. In 1806 Moore had published a collection of poems that was attacked for its immorality by Jeffrey in the *Edinburgh Review* in terms every bit as harsh as those Brougham used in dealing with *Hours of Idleness*. The result was that, when Jeffrey happened to be in London, Moore challenged him to a duel, although the meeting of the two men was then interrupted by the police before any damage could be done (duelling was, after all, against the law). When the pistols the combatants were to use were examined, one of them was found not to be loaded. This helped to attract a good deal of sarcastic press commentary on the whole affair, which Byron exploited in his own account. Who does not remember 'that eventful day', he asks, when Moore's 'leadless pistols met Jeffery's eye,/ And Bow-street Myrmidons stood laughing by?' (*CPW* I.244). In a passage at the centre of his poem, he imagines, in the mock-heroic terms so characteristic of *The Dunciad*, what the reaction in Edinburgh was to the possibility of Jeffrey being killed. The hill just outside the city known as Arthur's Seat, he says, was so disturbed that 'its steep summit nodded to its base' and the prison, which is inside Edinburgh and called the Tolbooth, would have felt 'defrauded of his charms,/ If Jeffrey died, except within her arms' (*CPW* I.244).

A biographer of Byron has called *English Bards and Scotch Reviewers* 'one of the most unpleasant poems in the English language'.[3] The temptation is to think that this is a judgement that could only come from someone who does not get out much, yet there are moments, as Byron was later to acknowledge, when his resentment and anger got the better of him. One of these concerns his guardian, the Earl of Carlisle, who had a few minor publications to his name. Byron had of course sent a copy of *Hours of Idleness* to Carlisle, who had done little more than return his thanks; but what more seriously upset Byron was his influential relative's failure to step forward when in March 1809 it was time for the young man to be inducted into the House of Lords. This involved a complicated and costly process of legal authentication, but everything became much simpler if an already-established House member acted as a sponsor. For some reason, whether because he was too busy or did not much like his young relative, the Earl of Carlisle failed to do this. The consequences are evident in lines Byron added to *English Bards and Scotch Reviewers*, more or less at the last minute:

> No Muse will cheer with renovating smile,
> The paralytic puling of CARLISLE:
> The puny Schoolboy and his early lay
> Men pardon, if his follies pass away;
> But who forgives the Senior's ceaseless verse,
> Whose hairs grow hoary as his rhymes grow worse? (*CPW* I.252)

The aggression in these lines, and several others like them in the same passage, is out of kilter with the prevailing tone of the poem as a whole and, as Byron himself rightly noted in 1816, 'the provocation was not sufficient to justify such acerbity' (*CPW* I.413).

Even when they are free of strong personal animus, there are lines in *English Bard and Scottish Reviewers* that could easily be considered mortally offensive by those against whom they were directed. Byron was aware that what he wrote might provoke a challenge, as Jeffrey's strictures on Moore had done; and since he was preparing to leave the country for a long period, he was anxious not to give the impression of someone who would cut and run. Even though his poem was only published two or three months before he left England, he made it clear that he was available to receive challenges before he sailed, and declared himself more than willing to take them up immediately, or at least as soon as he returned from abroad. He was never someone who sought to avoid conflict even when, however ridiculous the dispute between Moore and Jeffrey might be made to seem, duelling could be a life-or-death matter.

Byron's continuing struggle to manage his debts may have been one of the reasons he became anxious to move abroad, and doing so meant leaving Hanson and his mother to try what they could to clear up the mess. Another motive, apart from the restlessness of youth and a refusal to be deprived of what, in the past, was felt to be the privilege of all young aristocrats, might be found in the need he expresses to acquire the experience that would make him better qualified for a political career. He had not yet had time to address the Lords, and quite explicitly refused to ally himself with any particular party or faction; yet some kind of career in politics always remained possible.

Byron asked both Hobhouse and Matthews to accompany him on his trip but in the end only Hobhouse joined the party. Its other members included two manservants from Newstead as well as a young boy from there called Rushton, whom he had designated as his page and describes as a particular favourite of his. Quite what he meant by favourite is uncertain and hardly clarified by a teasing letter Byron wrote while he and Hobhouse were in Falmouth, waiting to embark, and sent to Matthews. Falmouth was a town, Byron wrote, surprisingly full of good-looking prostitutes, male as well as female. With accompanying classical references that lay the stress on homosexual rather than heterosexual love, he says, 'I have some intention of culling a handsome Bouquet to compare with the exotics we expect to meet in Asia' (*BLJ* I.207), indicating his belief, as he does several times in this short period, that 'Asia' was a place where sexual relations between men and boys were common and accepted. When he sent Rushton home from Gibraltar not with Fletcher, the younger of the two English manservants, but old Joe Murray, who had been the valet of his predecessor and to whom Byron was attached as a living reminder of the old days, it was because he felt that 'Turkey is too dangerous a state for boys to enter' (*BLJ* I.222).

Leaving his mother in charge of Newstead, Byron seemed to be turning his back, for a time at least, on the literary world. In *English Bards and Scotch Reviewers*, while announcing he was off to the Levant, he had promised, 'But should I back return, no tempting press/ Shall drag my journal from the desk's recess' (*CPW* I.261), making fun of a current fashion for travel literature. But that he would not report in some way on what he was about to see was unlikely given what an inveterate writer he was turning out to be. 'Always scribble, scribble, scribble! Eh, Mr Gibbon,' a member of the royal family is reputed to have said to the author of *The History of the Decline and Fall of the Roman Empire*, and scribbling was how Byron himself often described his own writing life, and what he was already spending much of his free time doing.

3
The Grand Tour

There had been a good deal of hesitation in Byron as to where he wanted to go on his grand tour. Western Europe was never on the agenda, much of it being out of bounds because of the Napoleonic Wars; but he sometimes talked of India and Persia, in addition to the region more generally known as 'the Levant'. In his promiscuous historical reading, he had become quite well informed on the Ottoman Empire and there was, in any case, at that time something of a 'Turkomania' that was reflected all over Western Europe in poetry, novels, plays and opera.

His original intention had been to take a ship straight to Gibraltar, so the Lisbon 'packet', or mail boat, was a second best. There were good reasons why communications between Britain and Portugal were reasonably common in this period. It was, after all, the time of what is known as the Peninsular War, when the British were attempting to resist Napoleon's total domination of Western Europe by establishing a bridgehead in Portuguese territory from which, with the help of the Portuguese themselves and Spanish freedom fighters, they could challenge his increasingly uneasy occupation of Spain. The close friend from Harrow who had joined the Coldstream Guards, and to whom Byron expressed his dislike of a military career, had been posted to Lisbon with his regiment but had drowned early in 1809 when his troop ship had collided with another vessel in the night.

There was no similar mishap to prevent Byron and his party landing in Lisbon on 7 July 1809. For the next year, much of where he went and what he did was recorded in meticulous (and often tedious) detail by Hobhouse in his diary, and more loosely, interestingly and intermittently by Byron himself in the first two cantos of *Childe Harold* (although he would not begin writing these until he was in Albania). In *English Bards and Scotch Reviewers*, he had made fun of those who were only too keen to offload diaries of their journeys as soon as they returned from abroad; and in his letters he is sarcastic about all the preparations Hobhouse was making for his 'forthcoming Book of Travels' (*BLJ* I.215). And yet a travel diary (in verse) is what *Childe Harold* partly is, and the descriptions in it of unfamiliar locations was one of the reasons for its popularity.

The two travellers did not think much of Lisbon, finding both its streets and inhabitants dirty; but they made some successful excursions beyond its limits. Only 25 kilometres (15 mi.) away, for example, was Sintra, which Byron in particular thought exceptionally impressive and beautiful, as he later tried to make clear in the first canto of *Childe Harold*. One place of interest there for Byron was the palace in which William Beckford, the wealthy author of *Vathek* (1786), had spent three years. *Vathek* was among Byron's favourite books and one which certainly had a very strong influence on his own writing. Usually classified as a Gothic novel, it does have supernatural elements; however, the setting is neither a medieval castle nor a monastery, but a caliph's court with harems, eunuchs, sherbets, houris and all the 'Eastern' paraphernalia long familiar from *One Thousand and One Nights*. The central figure, intended to be a religious as well as military leader, is very much an anti-hero who, in his search for more wealth and power, commits all the crimes that Beckford's impressively lurid, erotic and rich imagination can dream up, before finding himself, with his female partner, in a supposedly Muslim version of hell. Yet it was not only on account of this work that Byron was interested in its author. He had been excited when, on his way to Falmouth, he learnt his party had changed horses at the very inn where Beckford, 'the great Apostle of Paederasty', as Byron called him, had been staying the night before. Byron said that he tried unsuccessfully to meet this 'Martyr of prejudice' (*BLJ* I.210). What he meant was that Beckford's well-known bisexual nature had resulted in his sometimes choosing to live in exile.

In addition to being beautiful and home to Beckford, Sintra was known for the much more celebrated 'convention', or peace treaty, which bore its name. In 1808 the future Duke of Wellington, at the head of a combination of British and Portuguese troops, had won an important battle at Vimeiro which put paid to the French occupation of Portugal. Land victories against the French were uncommon enough to excite jubilation in Britain, but feelings quickly turned sour when two generals who outranked Wellington arrived in Portugal and concluded with Marshal Junot a partial peace treaty known as the Convention of Cintra (or Sintra), the terms of which were felt to be excessively favourable to the defeated enemy. In adding his voice to the criticism of the convention in *Childe Harold*, Byron demonstrated how he had the ability to make the verse form he had chosen for his poem (the nine-line Spenserian stanza) accommodate political satire just as easily as anything else.

When it was ready to leave Lisbon, the Byron party split up, with Fletcher and old Joe Murray taking the luggage by boat to Gibraltar while the others headed overland towards Cádiz, in the company of a local guide. This journey was the first demonstration of what a good international traveller Byron would be. Bed bugs and poor food seem rarely to have distressed him and he relished the physical effort of making his way on horseback through what became spectacular and difficult countryside at a rate that he claimed could be as much as 115 kilometres (70 mi.) a day. It was also a countryside in which the evidence of recent warfare was often clear. They could make Seville their principal staging post because the Supreme

Junta, or Spanish provisional government, was ensconced there; but in the following year the town would be retaken by the French.

There are a number of stanzas in Canto I of *Childe Harold* that describe this overland journey before moving into reflections on the pointless suffering warfare causes (several of these latter being added once the grand tour was over). Although not nearly as effective as the anti-war sections of *Don Juan*, they are interestingly associated with what Byron has to say about Spanish women in his poem's first canto. One immediate stimulus seems to have been seeing the Joan of Arc figure known as 'the Maid of Zaragoza' walking around Seville with the medals the Junta had awarded her pinned to her chest. In the siege of the city with which her name was always associated, and which had happened the year before, she had taken over the firing of a cannon when its male operatives had either been killed or fled, and inspired her countrymen to a successful counter-attack against the French. Her heroic behaviour reversed any idea of Spanish women as cloistered and inactive, decorative only, and Byron adds a further, more ambiguous note to this reversal in his elaborate description of the bullfight he and Hobhouse witnessed from a governor's box once they had arrived in the Cádiz area. Both of them found some aspects of this spectacle hard to watch, particularly the sight of the picadors' horses stumbling around the arena with their entrails leaking from their gored bellies. But Byron takes care to note that the excited and enthusiastic spectators included many young women.

That Spanish women were so different from those he had previously known may cause him some unease when it is a question of the bullfight, but not as far as relations between the sexes are concerned: 'Who round the North for paler dames would seek?/ How poor their forms appear! How languid, wan, and weak!' (*LB* 41). His observation of them in Seville and Cádiz led him to assume that they were hardly prudes – when a young Spanish woman prays to the Virgin, he slyly remarks, the object of her prayer is likely to be the only one present to deserve that title. He recognizes that what he claims to observe may have something to do with the war but, nursed as they are 'in the glowing lap of soft desire' (*LB* 43), the behaviour of Spanish girls nevertheless meets with his full approval.

At Cádiz, Byron and his party were able to board a navy frigate which took them to Gibraltar. It was there that Byron was reunited not only with his luggage but with Fletcher and Joe Murray. He then made arrangements to send the latter back to England along with young Rushton, having decided that Murray was too old for the likely rigours of the coming tour and that either the boy would not be safe in Turkish territory or his presence at Byron's side misinterpreted. From Gibraltar, he and Hobhouse sailed by packet boat to Malta, leaving there on 19 September in a small navy warship called *The Spider*, and arrived at Patras, in the Gulf of Corinth, a week later. Still skirting the main areas of conflict (the Ionian Islands, which they sailed past to reach Patras, would not be occupied by the British navy until a few weeks later), their subsequent itinerary seems to have been largely determined by what they heard from the various military and diplomatic individuals with whom they happened to travel, and the transport which happened to be available.

From Patras the two travellers might have been expected to press on towards Athens, but instead they sailed back to Prevas (now Preveza), on the coast of northwestern Greece, and from there made their way overland to Ioannina, where the English consular official welcomed them as the first compatriots he had seen there since his posting. This was territory well off the usual tourist track and an area controlled, on behalf of the authorities in Istanbul, by an Albanian warlord called Ali Pasha. He was anxious to conciliate the British, or play them off against the French, and had sent instructions for the visitors to be looked after and invited to his court in Tapeline, over the border in Albania itself. Byron's

Byron's Greece.

account of the journey to and from Tapeline, and what he found there, is one of the descriptive highlights in Canto II of *Childe Harold*. What seems to have particularly impressed him was the sound and sight of all the different kinds of soldiers, in their varied ethnic uniforms, milling around in front of Ali Pasha's palace. Shortly after their arrival, they were granted an audience with Ali Pasha himself, who displayed a graciousness quite at odds with his well-deserved reputation as a cruel despot. He told Byron that his aristocratic nature was evident in his small ears, an observation which their owner afterwards repeated in a manner that suggested he did not find the remark entirely absurd. There were no women to be found on the palace grounds, whereas, in lines omitted from the published version of the second canto, 'For boyish minions of unhallowed love/ The shameless torch of wild desire is lit' (*CPW* II.63).

Ali Pasha, who may have overestimated the political influence of Byron and Hobhouse, provided them with a guide to take them to Iaonnina (where Byron first began writing *Childe Harold*), and offered a ship, manned by his own people, for the journey back from Prevas to Patras. Byron's grandfather had happened to be the kind of vice admiral whose frequent misfortunes at sea had earned him the nickname 'foul-weather Jack'. His grandson's maritime experiences were on the whole pleasant, but this was the one occasion when his sailor's luck failed him. The Turks manning Ali Pasha's ship turned out to be incompetent and panicked when a storm split the mainsail and the mainyard snapped in two. The best that the few Greeks in the crew who happened to understand sailing could do was beach the ship north of Prevas, avoiding the neighbouring islands that were still held by the French. This experience convinced the two Englishmen that it would be preferable to head south by land, and when they were once again back in Prevas they managed to acquire an escort of around forty local soldiers since the territory they were about to cross was notorious for its bandits. It was in this way that they reached Missolonghi, from where they could take the short trip across the Gulf of Corinth back to Patras. No subsequent excursion in the Levant was quite as full of excitement and interest as this first one for Byron, who seems to have relished almost every aspect of it.

When it finally set out for Athens on 4 December 1809, Byron's party took a long way round so that the two classically educated

Englishmen could visit those sites whose names were already familiar to them. At this stage in their tour, two such places were Delphi and the mountain they knew as Parnassus. Settling in Athens a fortnight later, visits to the Acropolis gave Byron further thoughts on the relations between past and present with which he chose to open Canto II of *Childe Harold*. The general tenor of these is gloomy: seeing the ruinous state of various buildings on the Acropolis inclined him to those Hamlet-like reflections on the uselessness of human endeavour to which he was already prone. If the shrines of the great heroes and demi-gods of the past were no longer respected, what hope was there for the rest of us, especially if, as Byron at this point suspected, conventional religious notions of an afterlife had no foundation and the only conceivable species of immortality was that of living on in the minds of our successors? What the Acropolis represented for Byron was an 'Abode of Gods, whose shrines no longer burn', and the idea it prompted is that 'Religions take their turn' until 'Man shall learn/ Vainly his incense soars' (*LW* 54). In a note, which on the advice of Dallas he left out of his published poem, he is at pains to make clear that his scepticism is 'desponding not sneering'. But having seen in his travels 'the Greek and Moslem superstitions contending for mastery over the former shrines of Polytheism', his doubts about all three were increased. Besides which he feels that all the differing faiths have been more effective in making people hate rather than love each other, and he ends by singling out the Turks and the Quakers for praise because they at least are reasonably tolerant of other people's beliefs (*CPW* II.283).

It was not only time which had left the Acropolis in the state in which Byron saw it, nor solely warfare and neglect. An important contributory factor, in his view, was the large number of those from different European countries anxious to pillage what they saw of the art and architecture in Greece and take samples back home. Prominent among these was the Scottish peer Lord Elgin,

Louis Dupré, *Ali Pasha*, 1819, hand-coloured etching, aquatint and stipple.

for whose activities in Athens, and especially in the Acropolis, Byron developed an unusually strong antipathy. He expressed this in Canto II of *Childe Harold* and even more vehemently in a short poem in couplets which he wrote in 1811, the following year, called *The Curse of Minerva*. In this, the tutelary goddess of Athens, called Minerva by the Romans but known as Pallas Athena on her home territory, rains abuse on the 'Pict' who has done more harm to the city than even the Goths: 'So when the Lion quits his fell repast/ Next prowls the Wolf, the filthy Jackall last' (*CPW* I.324). It was, and occasionally still is, argued that by removing various friezes and other items from their original locations, sometimes with damaging force, Elgin was protecting them from further neglect or decay, and that by taking them to England he was allowing them to be seen by artists and art lovers who would not otherwise have the means to visit them *in situ*. But Byron would have none of this and increasingly sympathized with those Greek nationalists who regarded Elgin's activities as just one more humiliation that their so frequently conquered and occupied country had been obliged to suffer. In addition to this feeling was an unusually powerful sense of place in Byron, of wanting to stand on the exact spot where great events had happened in the past and see around him an environment which he could imagine as having been similar to the one the actors in those events might have experienced. Removing chunks of masonry from a structure like the Parthenon disrupted that possibility, and he was particularly incensed that, once Elgin had transported his spoils back to Britain, he attempted to sell them to the government.

Byron and Hobhouse arrived in Athens on Christmas Day 1809 and soon settled into a routine, making excursions on horseback to neighbouring 'classical' sites, such as the area where the crucial battle of Marathon was fought. In March 1810 the two friends profited from an offer from the captain of a British warship to take them to Smyrna, and then of another captain to carry them on to Constantinople (as Istanbul was then called). It was at the beginning of May 1810, therefore, on the second leg of this long excursion, that their ship was becalmed around the narrow entrance to what was known in classical times as the Hellespont. Byron was always inordinately proud of the feat he then performed, along with an officer from the ship in which he was sailing. As he often explained, the distance across the Hellespont is not much more than a mile but the currents make it more like four as far as swimming it is concerned (the two men failed on a first attempt). What made this feat so special for Byron, however, is the Greek myth in which Leander swam across the Hellespont in order to enjoy the favours of Hero, a priestess of Aphrodite, who lit a torch to guide him on his way and was devastated when a storm blew it out and Leander was drowned as a result. Although Byron testifies that swimming the Hellespont would hardly have left Leander much energy for love-making on arrival (not to mention the problem of

The Elgin Marbles, also known as the Parthenon Marbles, *c.* 447–438 BCE, in the British Museum, London.

swimming back), he was delighted to have demonstrated that it was possible and presumably, therefore, that the story may have had some foundation in fact.

Not far from the Hellespont, and from where his ship was moored, there was an area in which it was assumed the city of Troy once stood, but in 1796 a scholar called Jacob Bryant had argued that no such city had ever existed. 'I have stood upon that plain *daily*, for more than a month in 1810,' Byron wrote in 1821, 'and if any thing diminished my pleasure, it was that the blackguard Byrant had impugned its veracity. But I still venerated the grand original as the truth of *history* (in the material *facts*) and of *place*. Otherwise, it would have given me no delight' (*BLJ* VIII.21–2). Reminding people so often that he had swum the Hellespont, when several other of his swimming exploits were at least equally if not more noteworthy, could have been a way of reinforcing his belief in a reality that may have lain behind the myth.

Once in Constantinople Byron and Hobhouse were able to call on the British ambassador to Turkey and accompany him on a couple of occasions to an audience with the sultan. They added to the vivid local colour these occasions provided with excursions to nearby sites again familiar to them from their classical reading before, in July, setting off back again and docking in a port close to Athens. It was at that point the two men parted, Hobhouse having decided that it was time for him to return to England. Byron elected to stay on, often declaring that he was happier living abroad than he would be at home and that only the state of his financial affairs was likely to drag him back there.

At first, he felt the absence of Hobhouse as a relief, telling his mother on 30 July, 'I was sick of my companion (not that he was a bad one) . . . because my nature leads me to solitude' (*BLJ* II.9); and to Hobhouse himself he had written the day before, 'You cannot conceive what a delightful companion you are now you are gone' (*BLJ* II.7). Yet different as they were in temperament, they had got on reasonably well for a whole year. Reading Hobhouse's diary makes him seem dull, but perhaps Byron valued his stolidity as a counterbalance to what he recognized as his own mercurial nature. Certainly, he often listened to Hobhouse and valued his point of view. Posterity would later have reason to regret the authority Hobhouse could sometimes exercise, but there is perhaps already in their year together an anticipation of what its effect would be. It was while the two men were on their Albanian journey that Hobhouse persuaded Byron to destroy a prose memoir of his early life, presumably on the grounds that it contained revelations which would be harmful to his future 'reputation'.

It is sometimes suggested that Byron was glad to see Hobhouse leave because his departure gave him more freedom to indulge his sexual proclivities. There may be some truth in this even if letters he wrote to Hobhouse after he had left hardly indicate that Byron was secretive about what these proclivities were. On 22 June 1809, just before he was about to set out on his grand tour, the letter Byron had sent to his friend Matthews had included a reference to the 'Plen. And optabil. – Coit' to be found in Falmouth. L. A. Marchand's editor's note to *Byron's Letters and Journals* explains that the abbreviations in Latin refer to a passage in the *Satyricon* of Petronius where the original phrase is *coitum plenum et optabilem* ('complete intercourse to one's heart's desire'): the context there being the seduction of a boy. This same reference to Petronius occurs in a letter Byron wrote to Hobhouse from Patras on 4 October 1810 after his friend had left for home. 'Tell Matthews', he said, 'that I have obtained above two hundred pl & opt Cs and am almost tired of them,' and he goes on to explain, 'You know the monastery of Mendele, it was there I made myself master of the first' (*BLJ* II.23). On 20 November, but this time writing from Athens, he more or less repeats himself. 'Mention to M[atthews] that I have found so many of his antiques on this classical soil, that I am tired of pl & opt Cs' (*BLJ* II.29). Marchand seems to me right when he glosses the word 'antiques' as a reference to 'the ancient Greek penchant for boy love'.

After saying goodbye to Hobhouse, Byron was not back in Athens for long. Only a day or two later, he set out on the first of two trips to the western part of Greece known as the Morea (or the Peloponnese peninsula), which he had previously been invited to visit by Ali Pasha, whose son was governor there. Once back in Athens again, he formed a relationship with the teenager Nicolo Giraud, who was the brother of the wife or partner of Giovanni Lusieri, a Neapolitan painter often in Byron's company, despite being Lord Elgin's chief factotum in Greece. Nicolo became warmly attached to Byron, fulfilling the same role in his life as Edleston or Rushton had except that, in this case, the relationship was unlikely to have been platonic. When on a second excursion to the Morea in September 1810 Byron fell seriously ill with what he describes as a 'fever', Nicolo devotedly nursed him back to health before falling ill himself of the same sickness. The two were clearly very close: after Byron had decided in the spring of 1811 that he needed to go home, Nicolo accompanied him as far as Malta. He stayed with Byron on the island until the beginning of June, when there was an emotional parting of the ways.

Byron had completed a draft of the first two cantos of *Childe Harold* by March 1810, and was chiefly preoccupied with verse satire during his last months in Athens, in 1811. There was *The Curse of Minerva* but also a loose rendering into English of Horace's famous *Ars Poetica*. In Byron's time, as in the centuries before, a well-known distinction existed between satire that was in the manner of Juvenal, and therefore often biting and personal, and the more genial Horatian mode. Having been sufficiently Juvenalian in *English Bards and Scotch Reviewers*, and as he certainly is in *The Curse of Minerva*, Byron seems to have wanted to show that he could manage the Horatian mode also, even though in doing so he was inviting comparison with versions of the *Ars Poetica* by some famous predecessors, Boileau and Pope among them. On the whole his rendering is a success, although events back home would delay the publication of *Hints from Horace* (as he called his poem), especially as he insisted it should appear alongside the original Latin, and he would be dead before it appeared. Occurring in it is a tentative expression of his faith in the importance of literature: 'All, all must perish – but, surviving last,/ The love of letters half preserves the past' (*CPW* I.293). Although the general tone is moderate, there is the occasional shaft directed at contemporaries. An example would be the reference to the danger of any 'young Bard' sinking 'to Southey's level in a trice,/ Whose epic mountains never fail in mice' (*CPW* I.296), but then, as Byron had previously let slip in lines which he deleted in a proof copy, despite all the talk of the public service satire performs: 'Satiric rhyme first sprang from selfish spleen./ You doubt – see Dryden, Pope, St. Patrick's Dean.' (*CPW* I.293 notes)

Happily enough installed in Athens, it does appear that Byron would not have returned to England had his bank account been in good order. The occasional communications he had received from Hanson or his mother indicated why it was not, and he must have been especially concerned about a friend like Scrope Davies who, without any fortune of his own, had raised £6,000 on Byron's behalf in order to help him finance the grand tour and was coming under increasing pressure to pay it back. And he was not the only intermediary who was suffering from the difficulty Hanson had been experiencing in servicing Byron's debts, with the sale or better exploitation of his Rochdale property still held up by lawsuits.

During his voyage back home, Byron was not well. Apart from the effects of gonorrhoea, which he appears to have acquired from a prostitute in Athens, and haemorrhoids, he was suffering a recurrence of the fever that had recently struck him down in the Morea and which is now thought to be a manifestation of the malaria that would later lead to his death. He himself described it as what Mistress Quickly in *Henry v* calls 'a villainous "Quotidian Tertian"' and observed 'it killed Falstaff and may me' (*BLJ* II.44). There are scores of references in Byron's writings to Falstaff, in whom he seems to have recognized a kindred spirit. Dealing with illness must have helped engender the gloomy mood that is apparent in a memo Byron wrote to himself towards the end of May while he was still in Malta.

With that tendency he had to look back to a previous golden age of his life, Byron began his memo with the complaint that, at 23, the best of his existence was over. He then went on to say that having now had an opportunity to see mankind in many different contexts, he found it equally despicable everywhere. He described himself as 'sick at heart', no longer interested in women or boys, and noted that 'a man who is lame in one leg is in a state of bodily inferiority which increases with years and must render his old age more peevish & intolerable.' He noted that he was growing 'selfish and misanthropical', his financial affairs were in a bad state and he had outlived all his appetites and vanities, 'even this vanity of authorship' (*BLJ* II.47–8). He must have felt that he was coming home with problems no less acute than those which had bedevilled him two years before, and that all he had to show for the grand tour were three poems of whose value he was uncertain.

4

Fame

Once back on English soil, Byron did not exactly rush home to
see his mother. There were reunions with old friends, including
Hobhouse, and documents to sign at his lawyer's. It was only at
the beginning of August 1811 that he set off for Nottinghamshire,
and that was only because he had received a worrying note from a
local doctor stating that his mother was very ill. When he arrived
at Newstead, it was to discover that Mrs Byron had died the day
before. His relationship with her had always been fraught but it
was a shock to realize that, as far as close family was concerned, he
was now more or less alone in the world, although it was following
his mother's death that Byron re-established what was at least
correspondence with Augusta. Shortly afterwards, he received news
that an old 'favourite' of his from Harrow, John Wingfield, who
had joined the Coldstream Guards, had died abroad and also, more
devastatingly, that his close friend Matthews, who had recently
written to him and whom he was expecting to see soon, had
become entangled in weeds while swimming in the River Cam and
drowned. A little later, a letter from the sister of the individual he
had loved more than any other, John Edleston, informed him that
her brother had recently died of tuberculosis. This succession of
hammer blows was not designed to improve his mood and the grief
they occasioned found its way into the final revisions of the first two
cantos of *Childe Harold*, making its supposed protagonist, Childe
Harold himself, appear even more intriguingly melancholic.

At first Byron seemed less concerned to see these cantos in print than his adaptation of Horace. He gave them to the relative who had previously acted as his agent and Robert Dallas lighted on a publisher, John Murray, who was in many ways a strange choice since he belonged firmly to the Tory side of the political spectrum. The publisher of the *Quarterly Review*, which had been launched in 1809 to rival its Whig equivalent in Edinburgh, Murray counted among his advisors and associates several writers and polemicists who would have regarded Byron as politically beyond the pale. But he was a shrewd businessman and a rising star in the publishing world, and he and Byron would have a long and fruitful association. Their first exchanges began as they would go on, with Murray suggesting that *Childe Harold* would sell better if both its religious scepticism and its criticism of the Tory government's conduct of the war could be toned down, and Byron giving very little ground on either front.

The succession of deaths which had greeted Byron on his return to England might have made anyone else in similar tragic circumstances susceptible to spiritual conversion; yet he was proud of the fact that, when in Greece and suffering from the fever he felt would kill him, he had not sought help from religion. His former tutor and friend from Cambridge, Francis Hodgson, who was about to be ordained, seems to have chosen this moment to make what was by no means his first attempt at spiritual indoctrination, but was put firmly in his place by Byron, who questioned him strongly on the scapegoat system, which he felt was an important element in Christian theology. How unjust it was, he wrote, that the Son of God should have been 'sacrificed for the *guilty*. This proves *His* heroism; but no more does away with *man's* guilt than a schoolboy volunteering to be flogged for another would exculpate the dunce from negligence, or preserve him from the rod' (*BLJ* II.97).

By this time Byron's spirits were in any case improving, even if his money problems were not: a trip to Rochdale with Hanson had yielded nothing regarding the sale or exploitation of his properties there. What may have buoyed them up was the discovery that, with *English Bards and Scotch Reviewers* in its fourth edition, he was not entirely a back number in the literary world. One consequence of that work had been a letter which had been sent to him while he was abroad and he had therefore not previously seen. It was in this that Thomas Moore hinted at challenging him to a duel for having suggested his role in his dispute with Jeffrey had been ridiculous. Byron was perfectly willing to accept the challenge but a second letter Moore now wrote was conciliatory and the two men quickly became friends. It was Moore, therefore, who introduced Byron to Samuel Rogers, the rich banker poet around whom gathered a number of other prominent literary figures of the day, and to Lord Holland, although the latter connection was also established because at the beginning of 1812 Byron had decided to give his maiden speech in the House of Lords and Holland, who was to speak in the same debate, helped him with some of the preparations. These were quite extensive and reflected the ambitions Byron had nurtured at Harrow to be a great orator and play a significant role in his country's political history. The topic he chose for his speech was one he was well placed to discuss. There was considerable distress at the time in the Nottingham area among those in the hosiery trade who earned a living by weaving in the traditional way, so much so that there were riots in which the new and more efficient weaving 'frames', which had been recently introduced, were broken up. The Tory government, always unusually anxious about popular unrest following the French Revolution and its aftermath, decided to introduce a bill that made frame-breaking a capital offence. Helped by details which Holland and others provided, Byron spoke eloquently against this repressive measure, although, given how few left-wing Whigs there were in the Lords, and among the governing classes generally, to very little practical effect. Yet his contribution was admired by many in Whig

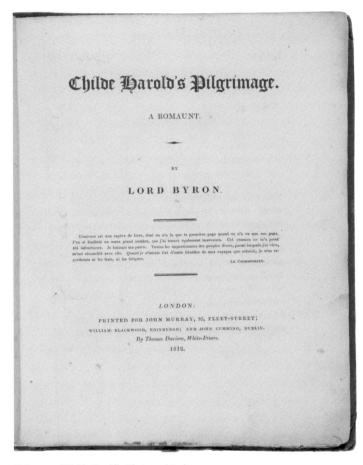

Title page of *Childe Harold's Pilgrimage* (1812).

circles and increased what one of today's publicists might call his
name recognition, although nothing to the same extent as that
resulting from the publication of *Childe Harold*, which followed
shortly after his maiden speech and was so immensely popular
that, as has often been said, it made him famous overnight.

That Byron now became one of those regularly invited to Holland House was one of the reasons he chose to suppress the fifth edition of *English Bards*, then in progress; but he was on the guest list of several other prominent Whig families. One of these was the Lambs. George Lamb was someone Byron had first known at Cambridge and was enough of a writer himself to have been made fun of in *English Bards*. But he was also involved in politics, although not as successfully as his elder brother William, who, as Lord Melbourne, would eventually become prime minister. William was married to a young woman called Caroline and it was with Lady Caroline Lamb that, in April 1812, Byron had a short but tempestuous affair.

Before that began, it had hardly been all quiet on the sexual front. At Newstead, Byron had turned to the familiar resource of the housemaids and particularly a new young girl from Wales named Susan Vaughan. But he was not a stereotypical Regency libertine in that his search for sexual gratification was often accompanied by a need for emotional attachment, for 'falling in love'. This helps to explain why, once he had moved from Newstead to London, and received from home verifiable rumours of Susan Vaughan sleeping with someone else, he was so cast down, attributing her 'faithlessness', as he always tended to in circumstances of this kind, to the fact that he had a club foot. It was on the rebound from Susan, as it were, that he began his affair with Caroline Lamb, thereby moving from what was practically the lowest rung of English society to its highest (Caroline, née Ponsonby, was a niece of the Duchess of Devonshire). There is no doubt that for a while the two were in love with one another, but Caroline more wildly, desperately and unpredictably than Byron, who, for all his liberal views, and in spite of the admiration he had expressed in *Childe Harold* for certain Spanish women, had highly conventional, conservative views about how the women with whom he was personally involved should behave. That there might be no great scandal in aristocratic wives having affairs was illustrated by Lady Melbourne, Caroline's mother-in-law, who was famous in her time for having had many. But what was essential was that they should be conducted with discretion, and an appropriate regard for the interests and reputation of the family in general.

Caroline was not discreet and had no respect for public opinion. Her behaviour at times was so eccentric that it began to alarm Byron and lessen his feeling for her. She lived with her husband in a large family mansion, the bottom floor of which was occupied by William's parents, Lord and Lady Melbourne. It was on Lady Melbourne that Byron now began to rely in order to handle what was becoming an increasingly difficult situation, and to whose charm, wit and intelligence he quickly became warmly attached. She was someone to whom he could reveal many of the secrets of his private life, knowing that, unlike his now absent real mother, she would not be disapproving or shocked but give him sage advice. It may well have been Lady Melbourne who was involved in persuading her son that he should take Caroline to a family estate in Ireland for a while so that she could calm down, and she encouraged Byron in his idea that he should look for some other object of romantic interest who might discourage Caroline from persisting in her attachment to him, even someone he could think he would like to marry. It so happened that the only one of the many marriageable girls he had seen at the parties to which, as the new star of the literary world, he was now regularly invited was the daughter of Lady Melbourne's brother. A much-cherished only child, Annabella Milbanke was a clever young woman who had a special interest in mathematics but had also written some poetry which had been passed on to Byron by Caroline for comment. Pious with a tendency to priggishness, she was a deeply serious person whom one would not have immediately identified as a suitable partner for Byron, even though he told Lady Melbourne that he had never seen a woman he '*esteemed*' so much' (*BLJ* II.195).

Thomas Phillips, *Lady Caroline Lamb*, *c*. 1810, oil on canvas.

But whether or not she was ideal did not at this stage much matter, since, having agreed to make a formal proposal to Annabella via the intermediary of her aunt, he found himself in October 1812 rejected, in part on the grounds of what she described to Lady Melbourne as 'the Irreligious nature of his principles'.[1]

This event appears to have caused less upset in him than her. Byron knew that, with considerable financial expectations if little immediately available money, Annabella was regarded as something of a prize in the marriage market while he himself had finally decided that the only way he could escape from his debts was by selling the Newstead estate. This was not a situation necessarily attractive to another aristocratic family and, besides, he was rapidly gaining a not unjustified reputation for immorality that his affair with Caroline Lamb, which Annabella must have known about, hardly lessened. She, on the other hand, was immensely flattered to have attracted the interest of the handsome young poet whom all her friends were discussing, and was perhaps privately convinced that he had many good qualities waiting to be brought out and strengthened by the right wife, some good woman who could save him from the bad habits into which he appeared to have fallen and, above all, from that lack of firm Christian belief which he took no trouble to hide. When she had first met him, earlier in 1812, she had noted in her journal that she was convinced Byron was 'sincerely repentant for the evil he has done, though he has not the resolution (*without aid*) to adopt a new course of conduct & feeling'.[2]

Another reason why it did not much matter that Lady Melbourne's niece was unable to provide an alternative to Caroline was because Byron had meanwhile found a new focus of his own. The Oxfords were one of the great families which his celebrity had now allowed him to meet. Like Lady Melbourne, Lady Oxford was well known for the number of her previous lovers, but whereas the former had just turned sixty, she was only in her early forties. So fond was Byron of Lady Melbourne that it is sometimes suggested he had sexual relations with her. If that is doubtful in her case, it is certainly true in that of Lady Oxford. After a period in Cheltenham, he retreated with her and her family to their country house in Presteigne, on the Welsh borders, where he became what he later learnt the Italians would call a *cavalier servente*. He seems to have been very happy there as he waited for the Caroline storm to pass. But she was not so easily reconciled to the affair being over: in

Ireland she had buttons made for her servants' liveries which read *Ne crede Byron*, which was his family's motto with an added 'ne'. She pursued him with letters, even sending one or two to Lady Oxford herself, having learnt that her former lover had now transferred his attentions to her.

The highly educated daughter of a clergyman, Lady Oxford appears to have taken all that Caroline could do to disturb her in her stride. Sixteen years older than her new lover, she provided Byron with that quasi-motherly comfort and security his nature often seemed to require. The influence she had on him did not mean that she was a passive figure. Politics was one of her consuming interests and she was more radical than any other of Byron's close female contacts, encouraging him not to let his political career fade away entirely. After his speech on the frame-breakers' bill, he had addressed the Lords on a proposal to change the legislation that prevented Irish Catholics from taking part in the government and administration of their own country. Apart from pleasing his new friend Thomas Moore, his intervention was no more effective than his support for the Nottingham weavers had been, and he may have been tempted to give up formal politics sooner than he did if it had not been for the encouragement of Lady Oxford. It was perhaps because of her that in June 1813 he agreed to support the right of a radical called Major Cartwright to carry on presenting petitions to Parliament for its reform.

No more effective in furthering change than his previous interventions, this speech of Byron's was the last time he spoke in the Lords, yet he was able to express his feelings more effectively outside the chamber in a number of political squibs, which he wrote and had published anonymously in the newspapers, an 'Ode to the Framers of the Frame Bill' being the first of these. It was while he was with Lady Oxford in Presteigne that Byron also exercised his satirical gifts in *The Waltz*, an attack on the craze for this new dance which he assumes was imported from Germany along with other things the country could do without, including the family of the Prince Regent. Like all the other Whigs, Byron found it hard to forgive the fact that when, on his father falling again into madness, the future George IV had assumed control at the beginning of 1811, he had turned his back on his former Whig friends and associates, transferring his support to the Tories.

These were all minor exercises for Byron's satirical powers and, with his *Hints from Horace* now very much on the back-burner, he must have been aware how much his current popularity depended on a quite different aspect of his gifts. In late 1812 he had begun putting together a narrative poem based on his Levantine experiences. While he and Hobhouse were in Albania they had heard a story about Ali Pasha which, affable as he then was with them, fully justified his fearsome reputation. One of his daughters-in-law had complained that his son was neglecting her for other women. After asking her to indicate who these women might be, he apparently had them all rounded up, sewn into sacks and thrown into the sea. That this was the official punishment for female indiscretion became clear to Byron in Athens when he met a group surrounding a woman who was being marched off to meet the same fate. With a combination of force and bribery, he managed to rescue her, although whether he knew who she was is not clear.

The poem Byron wrote is called *The Giaour* – the Turkish name for all non-Muslims, especially Christians – and the title refers to a young man who has been having an affair with a member of the harem belonging to a local caliph. He is not in a position to save her from drowning, an event which is assumed to take place in a gap between two fragments of the poem indicated by asterisks, but is able to ambush the caliph with the party of his supporters and kill him. This story of revenge is not what is most worthwhile in the poem, which occasionally descends into cliché and bathos: 'Who thundering comes on blackest steed,/ With slackened bit and hoof of speed?' (*LW* 212). Everything becomes more interesting in

Thomas Phillips, *Byron in Albanian Costume*, 1813, oil on canvas.

its second part, when the Giaour turns up in a local monastery and describes to a priest his depressed, guilt-ridden state while at the same time celebrating the love he felt for the drowned victim of the caliph's rage. His speech has the form of confession except that he neither expects nor wants absolution: 'Think me not thankless – but this grief/ Looks not to priesthood for relief' (*LB* 238). Although the verse form can sometimes make his words sound trite, they are on the whole impressive, and this psychological element, and further elaboration of what was quickly taking root as 'the Byronic hero', may have done as much if not more to make *The Giaour* a success than its more dramatic incidents and all the local 'Eastern' colour it sets out to provide.

Byron's difficulties with Caroline Lamb continued well into 1813, and one way of avoiding them, more radical than other attachments or even marriage, would have been to go abroad again. Almost from his first days back in England, he had made plans for doing this. He had returned to sort out his money problems and there seemed a prospect of doing this when Newstead was put on the market and a buyer came forward in August 1812 willing to offer £140,000. This massive sum would mean that he could rid himself of all his obligations, and invest the remainder in a way that would allow him to live in luxury in almost any foreign country he chose. But the potential purchaser began to get cold feet, and although he was eventually obliged to pay £25,000 in compensation, slowly pulled out.

That he would go abroad was nonetheless continually on Byron's mind and even more so because Lord and Lady Oxford had decided to do so. Without necessarily thinking he would travel with them – there were perhaps niceties to be observed – Byron aimed to join them in Sicily and then go back to the Levant. But his forward planning was as usual very indeterminate, and when in June 1813 Lady Oxford left the country it was without his having made the necessary arrangements for his own departure. The consequence was that he was again left without the direct emotional support he appears in this period to have always needed. It may have partly been because Lady Oxford's absence left him at what could be described as a loose end that Byron shortly began a flirtation with the young wife of a friend of his called Webster. He described why it never quite developed into an affair in a number of long and playful letters to Lady Melbourne in the latter part of 1813, making the whole situation sound like an extract from a comedy by one of the Restoration dramatists, or by Richard Sheridan, the Irish playwright and politician he admired enormously and would soon come to know well.

If Lady Melbourne was a keen recipient of Byron's lively descriptions of his relations with Webster's wife, it was because she was aware that, with Lady Oxford no longer in the picture, the Websters at least distracted him from entanglements which, for her, were far more serious and worrying than even the after-effects of the relation with Caroline. Five years older than her half-brother, Augusta Leigh had married a cousin and by the time Byron returned from his Eastern tour had three children by him. But Leigh was a gambler, and by 1812 the marriage was at breaking point. Augusta turned more and more to Byron in her difficulties, and after an actual as opposed to epistolary reunion in the summer of 1813, the two of them became very close. He had admitted to Annabella Milbanke that he 'could not exist without some form of attachment' (*BLJ* III.178) and, with their partly shared background and a similar sense of humour, Augusta began to assume a role in his life very like the one that had been played by the recently departed Lady Oxford. Trying to explain to Lady Melbourne why he had become so fond of his half-sister's company, he said that it was 'utterly impossible I can be half as well liked elsewhere – and I have been all my life trying to make someone love me – & never got the sort that I preferred before' (*BLJ* IV.104). One of the major differences between Augusta and Lady Oxford was that the former, with her yielding and affectionate temperament, was unlikely to urge him further down the path of radical politics than he was comfortable in going. Another difference might appear to be that of course, related as they were, they could not be sexual partners; yet it was precisely the broad hints in Byron's letters to Lady Melbourne that this is what they were which alarmed even that broad-minded correspondent, especially when one of his many further schemes for going abroad began to include taking Augusta with him.

Byron was not untroubled by the turn his life was taking and often relied on writing to relieve his anxieties, or express them indirectly: 'If it were not for some such occupation to dispel reflection during *inaction*', he wrote, ' – I verily believe I should very often go mad' (*BLJ* III.157). The latter part of *The Giaour* is related to his own periods of depression and in the second of his 'Eastern Tales', *The Bride of Abydos*, which is as equally exotic and outlandish as the first, he chooses to deal with what seems at first like incest. The son of a caliph is very fond of his sister, so much so that as the secret leader of a band of pirates, he is ready to save her from an unwelcome arranged marriage. In the course of the action, it is revealed that Zuleika, as this sister is called, is only his cousin, his own real father having been a brother of the caliph who was poisoned by him. This clarification removes the bar to further intimacy of the two young people, although this then fails to take place because, when Zuleika is having the situation explained to her, the young man is surprised by the soldiers of the caliph and killed while heroically fighting back, while she is too attached to him to survive his death. A location Byron had visited, notes which explain to readers certain Turkish titles or habits, some passages of quite fine writing and Byron's evident personal need to write about incest cannot save *The Bride of Abydos* from now seeming an immature fantasy, although one which did nothing to hinder his ever-growing commercial success.

The most usual way to indicate the extent of this success has been to note that the Eastern tale Byron went on to write after *The Bride of Abydos* sold 10,000 copies on the first day it was published in February 1814. This was *The Corsair*, a longer and more developed work, which, as the title suggests, also involves pirates. Its hero is Conrad, dour, guilt-ridden and resolute, but a natural leader of men. The one softness in his character is his devotion to Medora, who lives in a tower above the bay where the pirates are moored and is constantly looking out to sea every time Conrad and his piratical crew are expected to be heading home from one of their frequent forays. It is quickly revealed that he is about to undertake another of these, having just heard that a caliph of those parts (which are again those with which Byron had become familiar on his grand tour) is about to launch an attack on his stronghold. Conrad decides that it would be best to forestall him, but the consequence is another tearful farewell from Medora, who has nothing to do except anxiously await his return.

Arriving at the caliph's court, Conrad disguises himself as a dervish (not one of the whirling kind) and worms his way into his presence by pretending that he has been the pirates' prisoner and has just escaped. At an opportune moment, he throws off his disguise and, with those of his fellow pirates who have by now arrived, begins to attack the caliph's guard and set fire to his palace. Yet once it is in flames, he orders his men to save the women from the harem, making sure they come to no harm. He himself carries Gulnare, the caliph's favourite, to safety, giving the Turkish troops time to regroup and recognize how heavily they outnumber their attackers.

Conrad is eventually captured and thrown in jail while the caliph ponders the cruellest death he can imagine for him. He settles on impalement, but Gulnare has been moved by the honourable manner in which Conrad has treated her and, by bribing the guards, begins an effort to save him. On her second visit to his cell, she shows him a knife she has procured with which, on their way out of the building, he could kill the caliph as he is sleeping and thereby ensure that they will not be pursued. But Conrad would rather suffer impalement than exploit an unfair advantage over an enemy and is shocked when he realizes that, to make his escape certain, she is prepared to carry out the assassination herself. To his dismay, this is what she does, and although Gulnare, who has fallen helplessly in love with him, is beautiful, and has rescued him from an agonizing death, he cannot completely reconcile himself to a woman who is prepared to kill. She, on the other hand, has accepted that he is already committed to another woman in his pirates' lair, but when they arrive back there it is to discover that Medora has died, having pined away in the belief that Conrad must himself already be dead. Instead of then making do with Gulnare, as any coarse realist might have, Conrad disappears from the area and is never seen again.

Jerome McGann, perhaps aware of how melodramatic and unreal *The Corsair* could seem to more sceptical readers, claims that the poem 'is partly a symbolic formulation of the political situation of the day, as Byron saw it', with Conrad representing the 'equivocal forces of revolt' against the established powers (*CPW* III.445). That seems to me to give the work too much credit for seriousness, although his second claim, that the poem is best understood as a revelation of Byron's personal situation when he wrote it, is perhaps more sustainable, especially considering the clear links to his private life in the two earlier Eastern tales. Yet given that when Byron was writing all three, his relations with various women were extremely complicated, it is remarkable how conventional the attitudes to women are in this poem. Medora's only purpose in life seems to be to lavish uncritical love and attention on Conrad when he happens to be present, and yearn for his return whenever he is absent. Gulnare's character is more active but in a way which disqualifies her as a potential love partner. Given Conrad's situation, it seems ludicrous that he should be so concerned about Gulnare's proposed actions destroying his idea of what a woman ought to be; in depicting his attitude to her, Byron appears to have regressed from the moment when he recorded his admiration for the Maid of Zaragoza.

In *The Corsair*'s dedicatory opening letter to Thomas Moore, Byron refers to the various forms of versification that characterized his earlier, non-satirical poems, and in which he had demonstrated a remarkable facility. Announcing that the work which follows is in heroic couplets, he says in this letter that he wants to 'take my chance once more with the versification, in which I have hitherto published nothing but compositions whose former circulation is part of my present, and will be of my future regret' (*CPW* III.149). His principal reference here must be to *English Bards*, in the course of which Moore had been ridiculed. But in retrospect these words look like a temporary denial of what suited his talents best in favour of a style of writing that, immensely successful though it was at the time, was too jejune and shallow to last.

Shortly after *The Corsair* appeared, Augusta gave birth to a daughter, whom she called Medora and whose father might well have been her half-brother. Along with Byron himself, she had come to the conclusion that their situation was unsustainable and, like Lady Melbourne during the crisis with Caroline Lamb, was thinking of marriage as a way of ensuring that it was unlikely to continue or reoccur. She began writing to a friend whom she thought of as a likely possible wife for Byron, but, well before this, Annabella Milbanke, who by now had turned down several suitors and must have been wondering whether she had not missed a great opportunity by responding negatively to Byron's proposal, had taken the bold and unusual step, for a woman of her upbringing and character, of herself initiating another correspondence with him. The letter in which she did so is remarkable in tone, since she speaks of perceiving him surrounded by admirers who cannot properly value him. She says that she herself would have 'sought to rouse your own virtues to a consistent plan of action, for so directed, they would guide you more strictly than any mortal counsel', before entreating Byron to 'observe more consistently the principles of unwearied benevolence' and no longer suffer himself to be 'the slave of the moment'. In all she later suffered in her marriage to Byron, Annabella Milbanke was undoubtedly the injured party; but phrases like these indicate that she brought at least some of her difficulties on herself by entirely misconceiving his character and over-estimating the effect her own could have on him. Malcolm Elwin, the critic who has delved deepest into Annabella's affairs, has suggested that no one could have written them who had a sense of humour, and on this point the contrast with Augusta could hardly have been more marked. As Annabella herself was to write a year after she and Byron had separated, 'Augusta's society is a rare species of comic talent,' and she noted that her half-brother liked to boast, 'I can make Augusta laugh *at any thing*,' which was, she then added, 'a most melancholy truth'.[3]

Why Byron felt that he could not settle down and live with Augusta is obvious enough but it is puzzling that he continued to think of Annabella as his escape route, especially as he had described her as someone who 'seems to have been spoiled as a child – not as children usually are – but systematically Clarissa Harlowed into an awkward kind of correctness – with a dependence on her own infallibility which will or may lead her into some egregious blunder' (*BLJ* III.108). Ignoring the possibility that he would be the blunder, he continued to maintain that, of all the women he had seen, she was still the one he most liked and respected or, as he put it to Lady Melbourne, 'I do admire her as a very superior woman a little encumbered with Virtue' (*BLJ* IV.109). Annabella herself was in the awkward situation of having initially and falsely hinted at another attachment in order to make it easier for her to reject Byron, but now her efforts were on getting him to propose again without compromising herself. Yet he was once more planning an escape abroad, this time with his friend Hobhouse, who, having served some time in the militia in order to please his father, had recently returned from Ireland. Their aim was to visit Italy together but before they left Byron decided to try to clarify the situation with Annabella by asking her directly whether there was any possibility of a second proposal from him being more acceptable than the first. His letter was couched in defensive and relatively lukewarm terms, but she quickly returned an enthusiastic affirmative, which she sent to Newstead with a copy to Byron's apartments in London so as to be certain of reaching him. It was in fact on his estate, now restored to him after the failure of the sale, that Byron received her reply. According to Augusta, who was staying with him at the time, he ran his eye over its contents before handing it over to her and saying, 'It never rains but it pours.'[4]

5

Marriage

Whatever dismay Byron might at first have felt in realizing that he was now committed to Annabella Milbanke soon faded away and he reverted to his former belief that she could be his guide and saviour, someone who would lead him back to a more normal, respectable life. This was a heavy burden to place on a 22-year-old woman whose experience of life was much less extensive than his own; yet it was a role for which she could be said to have volunteered numerous times. The Milbankes lived in a village not far from Durham called Seaham, in northeast England, and Annabella had already invited him to visit them there. This was a trip which now became mandatory and, after a short time in London struggling with the details of a viable marriage settlement, Byron set out for Seaham on 29 October 1814, calling on Augusta at her home near Newmarket on the way. Aware of how impossible it would be to keep her half-brother to herself, she was pleased that Byron now showed signs of wanting to settle down and determined to do all she could to make the coming marriage work.

His first visit to Seaham was not a total success, but on the whole Byron and Annabella's relations at this point gave neither of them any strong feeling that they would be better calling the whole thing off, so Byron went back to London to continue his efforts to take the necessary financial measures for a reasonably rapid wedding. In broad, notional terms the idea was that Annabella would bring with her a dowry of £20,000 (with the expectation that when her

Walker & Boutall, after Charles Hayter, *Anne Isabella, Lady Byron*, 1812, photogravure.

maternal uncle, Lord Wentworth, died there would eventually be much more) while Byron generously settled on her £60,000. The trouble was that his future father-in-law's affairs were so embroiled that only a small portion of the £20,000 ever materialized, while Byron's £60,000 was dependent on Newstead being sold. Yet the potential for short-term difficulties did not prompt Byron to review his extravagant lifestyle or curb his tendency to impulsive generosity. In May of the previous year, with money available from the down payments from the man who had said he wanted to buy Newstead, he had sent Augusta £3,000 to help clear her husband's gambling debts.

Accompanied by Hobhouse as his best man, he arrived in Seaham just after Christmas in 1814 so that he and Annabella could be married on the second day of the new year. Self-conscious as he was, and with a hatred of fuss, Byron had insisted on a private ceremony, even going as far as obtaining a special licence which meant that the marriage could take place in the Milbankes' house, with an illegitimate but ordained son of the blue-blooded Lord Wentworth officiating. The couple then drove off to spend three weeks together in Halnaby Hall, a large house the Milbankes owned about 60 kilometres (40 mi.) away.

An accurate summary of Byron's subsequent disastrous twelve months of marriage is difficult because, whereas from his side there is comparatively little and certainly not much to indicate trouble, Annabella left behind a mountain of material known as the Lovelace papers. The problem is that much of this was written by either her or her relations shortly after she had left Byron and was attempting, through her legal representatives, to force him to sign a separation agreement while at the same time making sure that he would not feel in a position to demand custody of her recently born daughter. She therefore gave the impression that her relationship with him was doomed from the beginning, whereas it seems, from the letters of both, that there were at least periods when they got on quite well. Yet Byron had developed habits, in his eating and sleeping arrangements, for example, which would have imposed a burden on any partner, and Annabella no doubt had her foibles also. Although any marriage is likely to be in the first instance a clash of egos, in the opinion of a scholar who has explored the Lovelace papers in remarkable detail, Byron encountered in his new wife someone with 'an egotism more formidable than his own, in being unmitigated by imaginative sensibility'.[1] What he also suggests is that she took seriously everything her husband said and was not prepared, like Augusta, to laugh things off.

A possible sign that the Byrons' three-week honeymoon – or treacle moon, as he liked to call it – was not without its harmonious moments is the fair copies of items from *Hebrew Melodies* which Annabella made for him at that time. He had been approached by a Jewish composer to provide the lyrics for a number of songs to be based on passages from the Old Testament, the most well known of which today is perhaps the one that begins, 'The Assyrian came down like a wolf on the fold/ And his cohorts were gleaming in purple and gold,' which derives from 2 Kings 19 and Isaiah 37. This has a comparatively unfamiliar metrical pattern and used to be cited in school English lessons when the teacher wanted to say something about prosody. But not all the poems in *Hebrew Melodies* are based on the Bible, or solely illustrative of how effortlessly Byron could manipulate certain verse forms. At least two, for example, carry the false claim that they have been translated from French so that he can more freely express his complicated feelings about Napoleon, and the one which begins 'She walks in Beauty, like the night/ Of cloudless climes and starry skies' (*LB* 258–9), which is a beautiful poem and often anthologized, is a record of the fleeting impression made on him by the wife of a cousin he met at a social gathering.

Before buckling down to *Hebrew Melodies*, Byron had published in the August before his marriage what is perhaps the most successful of his early adventure stories in verse: *Lara*. Significant in this context because Annabella several times referred to it in her attempts to describe the strange ways in which Byron would often behave, *Lara*'s setting is not Eastern but some indeterminately feudal and possibly Spanish location where Lara is a landowner. He has returned to his estate from a period abroad and brought with him a devoted page, Kaled, as well as what seem like oppressive memories of previous ill-doing so that 'some deep feeling it were vain to trace/ At moments lightened o'er his livid face'. Having been 'Left by his Sire, too young such loss to know', he has become 'Chained to excess, the slave of each extreme', and accustomed to disguising his inner torments with humour so that he can seem 'gay amidst the gay', although people notice that his smile 'if often observed and near,/ Waned in its mirth, and withered to a sneer'

(*CPW* III.214–18 and 224). Canto I of *Lara* provides what is perhaps the fullest portrait to date of what became known as the Byronic hero, and to the extent that it could be regarded as a self-portrait (which its author always insisted was not very far), it is hardly a flattering one.

Invited to a gathering of local barons, he meets there a neighbour who has also recently been abroad and who hints at unspecified crimes for which he knows Lara to have been responsible. A combat between the two is arranged for the next day but the accuser fails to appear at the appointed hour, having been murdered, we later learn, probably by Lara himself. (At a loss to understand the hints of his own past guilt which Byron appears frequently to have let slip, Annabella Milbanke initially came to the conclusion that, while abroad with Hobhouse, her husband must have murdered someone.) The sudden disappearance of the man with information about Lara's past creates enough suspicion to alienate him even more from his peers and, when the peasants of the area begin to protest against the injustices they suffer, he assumes leadership of their revolt, having himself always been a model landlord. The lines describing how this leadership comes about are interesting in that they suggest Lara's sympathy with popular unrest has less to do with democratic feeling than hatred of his fellow landowners: 'And cared he for the freedom of the crowd?/ He raised the humble but to bend the proud' (*CPW* III.244). At first the revolt prospers, thanks in part to Lara's courage and popularity with his followers, but eventually it is put down and he is killed, refusing as he dies the consolations of religion. In a final *coup de théâtre*, Kaled, who has been at his side throughout the action, turns out to be a girl from the East in disguise.

Byron may have killed someone during his grand tour, but it seems highly unlikely, and there were reasons for his feeling uncomfortable which lay much nearer home. It was unfortunate for his marriage that there was no avoiding Augusta. Having returned to Seaham, the couple were then duty or at least convention bound to visit Byron's sister on their way south to London; and when Augusta managed to secure an appointment as one of the ladies-in-waiting to the queen (which her financial situation hardly allowed her to turn down), Annabella invited her for an extended stay in the house the Byrons had rented in Piccadilly, in spite of her husband's fairly strenuous indications that this was not a good idea. His opposition did not of course come from dislike of his sister (quite the contrary), but he was conscious of the tensions which arose when the three of them were together. Annabella was soon made aware that he seemed to prefer Augusta's company to her own, but it was months before she began to suspect that the intimacy they enjoyed was anything more than what many blood relations manage to achieve. Not at all secretive by nature, Byron dropped heavy hints as to what the real situation had once been (there are no suggestions it continued after his wedding), and occasionally complained that their marriage would have been so much more appropriate had it taken place when he had first proposed. Annabella interpreted these last remarks as a mean-spirited manifestation of injured pride, as if he were punishing his wife for saying no in the first instance, and it certainly has that appearance. It was a long time before its deeper meaning crossed her mind. She must have known about his affair with Caroline Lamb, and had probably also heard at least rumours about Lady Oxford, but that he could have slept with his own sister was an idea so foreign to her pious nature that she was not quick to take it up.

Apart from the remorse Byron felt about what had gone on with Augusta before his marriage, there were also pressures on him of a more ordinary kind which helped motivate his often bizarre and, from Annabella's point of view, alarming behaviour in their time together. The house he had agreed to take in London used up all of her annual income in rent (around £700), and in setting it up for married life he must have spent money very freely despite still owing, at this juncture, £30,000 to various creditors. As a member of the House of Lords he could not be arrested for debt, but this did not mean he was not continually harassed by those to whom he owed money and, by November, when Annabella was into her seventh or eighth month of pregnancy, there was at least one bailiff sharing the house with them. Matters ought to have been improved by the death of Lord Wentworth earlier in the year, and the reversion of his large income, which was eventually destined for Annabella, to Byron's mother-in-law; but although the Milbankes tried to raise money on his wife's expectations there were legal complications which prevented them from being able to help. When before his wedding Byron had heard that Annabella's father was in financial trouble, he had taken no notice, repeating his insistence that he was not marrying her for her money; but if his own mother had been alive, she might well have pointed out that the woman he had chosen was hardly the 'golden dolly' he needed to rescue him from his situation.

An indication of how pressing Byron's money troubles became is that he decided to sell his library. When his publisher got wind of this, he offered Byron an immediate £1,500 and said he could have an equivalent sum ready shortly. But Byron refused to accept any help even though he must have known that Murray had been making a great deal out of his work, and he himself had only recently broken his gentleman's rule of never writing for profit by accepting £700 for *Lara*. He was still 'scribbling', producing in this period two short verse narratives, *The Siege of Corinth* and *Parisina*. The first dramatizes an event that had taken place in the war between Venice and the Turks at the beginning of the eighteenth century and features a Venetian who, much like Coriolanus, is so offended by his treatment at home that he helps lead an attack against his own people holed up in Corinth, refusing to desist even when the ghostly figure of a Venetian lady he loves appears from out of the besieged city and asks him to do so. Its chief interest lies in the psychology of someone whose pride, like Lara's, prompts him to become an enemy of his own particular class. The subject-matter of *Parisina*, by contrast, seems closer to home. This poem is also based on historical records, but those of Renaissance Italy rather than the Levant. A fifteenth-century Italian aristocrat discovers that his beautiful wife, the Parisina of the title, is having an affair with his much-loved illegitimate son. The man orders his son to be beheaded and the wife disposed of in ways which Byron does not make clear. The relations of the two guilty lovers qualify as incest, which, he says in a preface, might be deemed by some a subject 'unfit for the purposes of poetry', yet 'the Greek dramatists, and some of the best of our old English writers, were of a different opinion.' He goes on: 'As Alfieri and Schiller have also been, more recently, upon the Continent' (*CPW* III.358). This short, sad tale is told in a relatively straightforward manner, although not without a touch of that gruesome element which was often present in the Gothic novels of the time, and is perhaps one of the reasons for their popularity. When he was walking around the walls of the sultan's harem in Constantinople on his Eastern tour, Byron had seen dogs eating a human corpse, and, in *The Siege of Corinth*, he favours his anti-hero with this same experience when he is circling the town he is about to attack on the following day. In *Parisina*, the execution of the bastard son is described in some detail until the moment when 'His eyes and lips a moment quiver,/ Convulsed and quick – then fix for ever' (*CPW* III.371).

For *The Siege of Corinth* and *Parisina*, taken together, Murray offered 1,000 guineas, but Byron, doubtful that the tales were worth publishing on their own, and still uneasy at becoming a professional writer rather than one of the 'mob of gentleman who wrote with ease', as Pope had put it, refused the offer. A little later, however, friends suggested to him that there were writers in need to whom this money might be diverted and he fell in with a scheme whereby a little more than half of the sum Murray was offering should be given to the radical novelist and philosopher William Godwin, and the remainder divided between Charles Maturin (later to be the author of a successful Gothic novel of 1820 called *Melmoth the Wanderer*) and Coleridge. But to Byron's considerable anger and dismay, Murray demurred. He may reasonably have thought that it was up to him to decide where his money should go or, as a Tory surrounded by Tory advisors, objected to subsidizing Godwin, whose books were much admired by those on the radical Left. At the same time, he may well have been baffled by the aristocratic pride which prevented Byron acknowledging that one of the writers in need was himself.

Coleridge was later to receive £100 from Byron for a play he never managed to complete. They had got to know each other through Byron's acceptance, in June 1815, of a position on the managing committee of Drury Lane. Always interested in drama, the opportunity to take an active part in managing the newly rebuilt theatre must have been a welcome distraction from troubles at home, and he worked hard at reading scripts and trying to find new playwrights. The Drury Lane connection was one Annabella must have soon regretted as it seems to have encouraged the heavy drinking that became part of her husband's pattern of behaviour in the second half of 1815 (another member of the managing committee, Douglas Kinnaird, was an old friend and drinking companion); and it also facilitated his taking a mistress from among the actresses more or less in the period when she was preparing to give birth. Although Annabella testified that Byron rarely if ever manifested any violence towards her, the effects of remorse centred around Augusta, his increasing money problems and a great deal of brandy produced behaviour and whirling words so extreme and disturbing that she took refuge in the idea that he must be going mad and secretly called in a doctor in the hope of having him certified. This would mean that she would be able to have him put under physical restraint and, for example, prevent him from taking that extended trip abroad he was now sometimes threatening. But the doctor in question, ostensibly called in to deal with various physical ailments from which Byron was suffering at this time (many of them connected with a digestive system damaged by years of eccentric dieting and now further by his drinking), came to the disappointing conclusion, for her, that in his meetings with her husband he showed no signs of being anything but sane. Madness would, for Annabella, have been an explanation for conduct which she otherwise found unaccountable, rock solid as she was in her conviction of having always been a good wife.

There had been a loose agreement between the Byrons that once their baby was born, Annabella would go to her parents to recuperate. On 15 January 1816 he said goodbye to his wife and daughter and was never to see them again. Once Annabella began to describe to her parents how she had been treated in London, they were appalled and declared she could never go back to living with Byron, a resolution she quickly came to share. Her father wrote to his son-in-law with proposals for an amicable legal separation, which, partly because Annabella had exchanged affectionate words with her husband before leaving, took Byron completely by surprise. Hobhouse, who came up to London at this time in order to offer his support, testified to how distressed and upset his friend was made by the situation; and in a number of letters Byron then wrote, he pleaded with Annabella to come back to him. Believing that his wife must have been pressured into making this move by those around her, he asked for a meeting, which she refused, and a confirmation that a separation was her own wish, which she duly supplied. His first instinct was to resist so that, aware in particular that it might not be easy to deny a lord control over his child, Annabella and her party began to assemble both a formidable legal team, which would eventually include Henry Brougham, the reviewer who had thought so little of *Hours of Idleness*, and evidence of Byron's various crimes and misdemeanours. It is to this period that many of Annabella's accounts of his mistreatment of her belong.

Naturally defiant, Byron's determination not to lose his wife and daughter without a fight must have been hampered by his awareness of how increasingly difficult his sister's position was becoming. Augusta had stayed on with him after Annabella had left and was working hard to both calm her brother down and effect a reconciliation. At no point did Byron claim that his wife's conduct had been anything other than exemplary, and he was ready to give all kinds of undertakings about his own behaviour in the future. But her attitude hardened with the passage of time, and she was now more or less convinced that he and Augusta had been sexually involved before her marriage. This was not information that her legal team necessarily intended to use in any coming court battle, but it could be fed into the aristocratic rumour mill in ways that would threaten Augusta's position at court, and her reputation generally. The same could be said of details about Byron's homosexual activities in Greece – and allegedly also at home – which were now obligingly provided by Caroline Lamb, who reappeared on the scene once news of the separation began to circulate. As far as the strength of Byron's position was concerned, these provided a threatening background to the testimonies Annabella's lawyers were soon collecting from servants, and other members of the Byron entourage, about how badly he had treated her.

He was of course an immensely popular author, with what could be described as a cult following, but his portraits of men with dark secrets in their past were hardly a help in his present situation, and the praise he had received was in any case by no means universal. There were always those who from the beginning had objected to his attitude to Christianity (Annabella included), and he had made bitter political enemies along the way. When Napoleon had first been defeated and sent to Elba in April 1814, Byron had written an

George Cruikshank, 'The Separation, a Sketch from the private life of Lord Iron who Panegyrized his Wife, but Satirized her Confidante!!', *c.* 1816, engraving.

ode which showed that his support for the former French emperor had become equivocal in that his poem deplored the fact that he had not fallen on his sword, as any true hero should, but lamely accepted defeat. Yet he was excited by the almost miraculous way Napoleon was able to escape from his island prison and regain control of France, and would no doubt have liked to have accompanied Hobhouse when he went over to Paris in order to observe what became known as 'the hundred days'. The conclusion of the Napoleonic adventure at Waterloo in June 1815 produced an almost universal outburst of patriotic fervour in Britain in which Byron could not share, although not because he was anxious to witness more conflict. What he detested was the idea of former kings and emperors being able to re-establish themselves in countries that had benefitted from being governed in a more just and equitable manner under the Napoleonic code, in spite of all the manpower and money they had been obliged to provide for its author's constant wars.

Whatever public support Byron enjoyed waned considerably on the appearance of two poems in which he expressed his feelings about his plight – let off steam, as it were. These had been published privately in a limited edition of fifty copies but Henry Brougham was instrumental in having them appear in a newspaper called *The Champion* (having benefitted from the celebrity which the recent rapid expansion of newspapers and journals facilitated, it was perhaps only fair that Byron should now experience its downside). One of these poems was written shortly after he had, very reluctantly, signed the separation agreement and was in the form of a goodbye to his wife. 'Fare thee well,' it begins and goes on to promise that 'Never/ 'Gainst thee shall my heart rebel.' Yet what follows is in fact full of self-pitying reproach:

> Though my many faults defaced me,
>   Could no other arm be found,
> Than the one which once embraced me,
>   To inflict a cureless wound! (*LB* 262)

The second poem must have seemed even more of a mistake in retrospect. It concerned a woman who, having been Annabella's governess, became her maid and confidante. Wrongly convinced that his strong-minded wife must have been under the sway of others in order to act as she did, Byron blamed this woman, Mary Clermont, for many of his troubles and launched an attack on her which was rightly regarded as vicious and unworthy. Reproaching her for the rise from modest social origins which has allowed her to dine 'off the plate she lately washed', he says she is like some snake who steals 'within your walls/ Till the black slime betrays her as she crawls', calls her a 'hag of hatred' and claims that when she is dead, 'Even worms shall perish on [her] poisonous clay' (*CPW* III.382–6). There is clearly in this poem a good deal of diverted anger which he felt inhibited from expressing towards Annabella herself, although

'Fare thee well' does include the idea that although his wife may be the 'Serenely purest of her sex that live', her one weakness is not knowing how to forgive: 'Too shocked at faults her soul can never know,/ She deems that all could be like her below.' When she was leaving London with her baby, Annabella had written to Byron an affectionate note, which begins 'Dearest B' and says, 'Don't give yourself up to the abominable trade of versifying – nor to brandy – nor to anything or anybody that is not *lawful* and *right*.'[2] The injunction against versifying should perhaps have been one Byron obeyed in the case of these two poems, since they did him no good in the realm of public opinion and whipped up a storm of criticism that made him even more eager than usual to shake the English dust off his feet as quickly as possible.

He had been itching to go abroad again after his return from the East and even raised the possibility of a foreign excursion with Thomas Moore a few weeks after his marriage, with or without their wives. In one sense, therefore, Annabella and his English critics could be said to be doing him a favour, but of course he did not see it that way. There was a difference between leaving a country of one's own accord and leaving accompanied by a storm of criticism and abuse.

In the few weeks before he was ready to set off, Byron made an important new contact. Like those who crowd around a rock star at the stage door, there were many women who would have liked nothing better than getting to know Byron. Usually he was sensible enough to ignore their approaches, but the letters he received from a young teenager called Claire Clairmont were too intriguing for him to brush aside. The daughter of the woman who had become William Godwin's second wife after the death of his first – Mary Wollstonecraft, author of *A Vindication of the Rights of Woman* – Claire had left the Godwin household after her stepsister, Wollstonecraft's daughter (also called Mary), had run off to live with a young poet and political firebrand recently sent down

Amelia Curran, *Claire Clairmont*, 1819, oil on canvas.

from Oxford for publishing a pamphlet entitled *The Necessity of Atheism*. This young man was, of course, Percy Bysshe Shelley, who could not yet marry Mary Godwin because he was still married to someone else and who welcomed Claire into his household. Sexual liberation had been one of the themes of Godwin's philosophical writing but he was not at all pleased to lose his favourite daughter in this fashion, while Claire showed his lessons had been imbibed by herself, as well as her sister, in directly suggesting to Byron convenient ways in which they might sleep together. She also succeeded in discovering that his plan was to head for Geneva in the first instance and wait for Hobhouse to join him there before travelling on to Italy. Shelley and Mary Godwin were also planning a trip abroad at this point, but it was largely thanks to Claire, whose presence with them had become a matter of course, that they also decided to make their way to Geneva.

Byron's preparations for what would turn out to be a permanent exile were elaborate. One of the spoils of Waterloo had been the capture of Napoleon's coach. Byron had one built along the same sumptuous lines at a cost of £500 (it was only after his death that it was completely paid for). For some time, Fletcher had been re-engaged as his valet and he now again recruited Rushton from the Newstead estate, although he was to send him back home before he left Geneva. During the year of his marriage, and in the latter part especially, he had been continually unwell, so decided it would be useful to be accompanied by his own private doctor. The young man he chose was called Polidori and just out of the Edinburgh medical school, but he had literary antecedents which may have made him seem a particularly appropriate choice: his father had been the secretary of the Italian poet Alfieri before emigrating to England to teach his native language. That his son was also an Italian speaker may well have added to Byron's sense of his suitability, although Hobhouse took an almost immediate dislike to Polidori, as he did to almost anyone who might be able to establish a closer relation with his old friend than he himself already had. Engaging in addition a Swiss guide called Berger, and with his separation from Annabella now confirmed, the Byron party left England on the 25 April 1816 and landed in Ostend on the following day.

6

Switzerland

Travelling through Belgium to Cologne and then down the Rhine
into Switzerland was not the quickest route to Geneva, but Byron
had, or at least anticipated having, difficulties in acquiring the
necessary travel documents for entering France – and in any event
he was reluctant to set foot on French soil now that the Bourbons
were back in charge. His party needed two coaches, which was
fortunate since the one he had just had made broke down and,
although Brussels had not been on his itinerary, they had to stop
off there to have it repaired. Once he was in the Belgian capital, it
seemed inevitable that he should visit what had quickly become
a prime tourist site for the English, the battlefield of Waterloo,
ambivalent although he felt about the defeat of Napoleon. A
description of what he experienced on treading the ground where
many had died so recently became the first set piece in what would
be Canto III of *Childe Harold*, which, now he was on his travels
again, and to his publisher's delight, he had begun to write.

Byron began this poem with an address to his lost baby
daughter ('Is thy face like thy mother's, my fair child!/ Ada! sole
daughter of my house and heart'), an open appeal for public
sympathy which cannot have pleased his wife. That he went on
to present himself as someone whose latest misfortune in being
deprived of his family only increased the hopelessness that he
was always inclined to feel made it easy for him to blend this
idea of himself with the persona of Childe Harold, the man who

has 'grown aged in this world of woe,/ In deeds not years', whose 'springs of life' were poisoned early, and who had learnt that 'life's enchanted cup but sparkles near the brim' (*LB* 104–6). As Walter Scott remarked after reading Canto III, Byron had 'more avowedly identified with his personage than upon previous occasions, and in truth does not affect to separate them'.[1]

The reflections on Waterloo which the poem then quickly moves into are full of confused feeling. On the one hand Byron wanted to celebrate the bravery of those British soldiers who had died there, one of whom was his cousin, but on the other he was convinced that this was a 'king-making victory' and, politically speaking, Europe was likely to be much the worse for it. As he continued his journey, Byron would come across a battlefield which, more safely in the distant past, raised a much less complicated response. Moving down the Rhine from Cologne, with its picturesque littering of ancient ruined buildings along its shores ('chiefless castles breathing stern farewells'; *LB* 117), his party came through Basel and Bern to eventually reach Morat, where, in the fifteenth century, a confederation of Swiss states had heavily defeated the army of the Duke of Burgundy. This was easier for him to think about because, apart from having happened a long time ago, the battle could be regarded as a triumph of republicanism over autocracy. From Morat, it was not far to Geneva and the Hotel d'Angleterre, where all the more well-to-do British travellers stayed, and where Claire Clairmont was anxiously awaiting his arrival.

Still only eighteen, Clare was oscillating uneasily between an acknowledgement that the way in which she had offered herself to Byron meant she had no right to criticize his behaviour, and resentment at the cavalier fashion with which he had already, and would in future sometimes treat her. Because she was the main reason why Shelley, her half-sister Mary and their baby son William were in Geneva, she was beginning to wonder whether Byron had deceived her in saying he would be heading there. It was late on Saturday 25 May that his party did finally turn up, but she was upset that he did not immediately get in touch. On the Monday morning she wrote him an angry note in which she said how unkind and cruel she thought he was in treating her with such 'marked indifference', and then added that if he would meet her on the top floor of the hotel that evening at 7.30, she could conduct him to her room. As Byron was later to write to Augusta, despite all the rumours circulating, he had had only one mistress while he was in Switzerland and he 'could not exactly play the Stoic with a woman – who had scrambled eight hundred miles to unphilosophize [him]' (*BLJ* V.92).

Crucial to Claire's plans was that Byron and Shelley should enjoy each other's company, so she was relieved that they hit it off more or less immediately. They had similar educational backgrounds, although it was Eton and Oxford in Shelley's case; and both had reasons to feel that they were the victims of an English moral establishment, of 'cant' as Byron would become used to calling it. It helped that Shelley admired the older poet greatly and felt the success he had achieved was deserved, while Byron must have become aware of how much more of an intellectual Shelley was than himself, astonishingly well read and a better classicist. But all this could have been true without fostering the close and warm friendship that quickly developed and which was not, at this early stage, hampered by any envy on Shelley's part or an awareness in Byron that his new friend's convictions on politics, religion and sexual liberation were far more determinedly radical than his own.

Neither of them was comfortable with either the expense of the hotel or with what they must have felt were the disapproving glances of their compatriots also staying there; and it cannot be an accident that they soon found houses to rent which were close to each other. This was in a village called Cologny, eastwards along the lake shore from Geneva itself. The Shelleys, as it is convenient to call them, took a house quite near the water called the Maison

Chapuis while Byron chose a villa at least three times as big, which was further up the steep slope that led from the shore and was known as the Villa Diodati. But there was less than ten minutes between the two. Before leaving the Hotel d'Angleterre, both Shelley and Byron had acquired boats so that a routine now began of sailing on the lake, having meals together and long conversations often stretching well into the night.

One surprising result of these conversations would seem to be four well-known stanzas in Canto III of *Childe Harold* in which Byron, having brought his protagonist to Geneva, describes what it feels like to be drifting in a boat on its lake, surrounded by Alpine scenery. 'I live not in myself,' these begin, 'but I become/ Portion of that around me, and to me,/ High mountains are a feeling' (*LB* 125). Previously Byron had been an observer of Nature but now he describes himself as absorbed into it. When Wordsworth read these lines he recognized them as derivative of his own poetry, in particular 'Tintern Abbey'. Byron had previously made fun of Wordsworth, not only for his 'simplicity' but for what he regarded

The Villa Diodati today.

Alfred Clint, after Amelia Curran and Edward Ellerker Williams, *Percy Bysshe Shelley*, *c.* 1829, oil on canvas.

as his mysticism, which he claimed not to understand. But Shelley appears to have convinced him that there was much more to the older poet than he had previously thought and momentarily turned him into a lover of Nature along Wordsworthian lines, although, as the four stanzas proceed, his own influence is also apparent. Militant atheist though he may have been, Shelley was a fervent believer in the spirit world. A little less fervent, Byron nevertheless now looked forward to the time when he would be disembodied, no longer a 'link reluctant in a fleshy train', and wondered if he would not then merge into 'bodiless thought? The Spirit of each spot?/ Of which, even now, I share at times the immortal lot?' How could being 'reft of carnal life' mean permanent extinction, he suggests, when the mountains, waves and skies are 'a part of me and of my soul, as I of them?' (*LB* 126). A sceptic as far as Christian belief in the afterlife is concerned, this is the closest Byron would come to denying that death is the end of all and different from the idea that the only species of immortality is in the mind of others.

Sailing on the lake was dependent on the weather and unfortunately the summer of 1816 was to go down in meteorological history as one of the very worst on record. There had been in Indonesia a massive volcanic eruption which threw millions of tons of dust into the upper atmosphere and was assumed to be the cause of why, day after day, the sun was veiled and harvests everywhere were ruined. There were therefore many early summer days in Cologny when it was too cold and miserable to go out and the Shelley party would join Byron and Polidori in Diodati to amuse themselves as best they could. It was on one of these occasions that Byron suggested there should be a competition as to who could tell the best story involving some aspect of the supernatural or uncanny. His own contribution was a tale of a gentlemanly vampire, which Polidori was later to develop and publish, but the undoubted winner was Mary Godwin, who came up with the beginnings of what would become, with Shelley's help,

Frankenstein. In June 1816, though she was still not yet nineteen, she was the mother of a five-month-old baby fathered by Shelley, whom she would go on to marry after his first wife, Harriet Westbrook, drowned herself in the Serpentine at the end of the year. From this distance in time, she seems like a quiet, reserved young woman, somewhat in awe of both her brilliant lover and the charismatic and celebrated Byron; but what she first sketched out in those meetings in Diodati would become a work at least as well known as anything the two men ever wrote.

When the weather improved a little towards the end of June, Byron and Shelley seized the opportunity to take the boat trip around Lake Geneva they had been planning. This was to be dominated by thoughts of Rousseau, whom they both admired, in particular if not exclusively for his sentimental epistolary novel set in the Lake Geneva area, *Julie, ou la Nouvelle Héloïse*, a tale of hopeless love and noble suffering which had become immensely popular all over Europe after its first publication in the 1760s. One of the lakeside towns which features in this work is called Meillerie, and it is as they were sailing away from there for their next port of call (Saint-Gingolph) that Byron and Shelley ran into a violent storm. So bad was it, and so incompetently did the local who was sailing the boat for them handle the craft, that there was a serious likelihood of capsizing, and then drowning, only a few hundred yards from the rocky shore. Byron already liked and admired Shelley but both feelings were strengthened by the complete sangfroid with which the younger man, who could not swim, ignored Byron's explanations of how he could save him once they were in the water, and calmly accepted what looked like his future fate with folded arms.

When the boatman finally managed to regain control of the sails and make it into Saint-Gingolph, Byron was able to see that the wind had uprooted several huge trees in the higher ground above the village. It may have been this escape from a life-threatening situation that prompted Shelley, when he was in the local inn that night, to make a will, with Byron as a witness. He was distributing large sums of money which he expected to receive once his father had died, an event he cannot be expected to have anticipated would take place long after he himself was dead. His chief concern was to make provision for Mary, whose situation as the unwed mother of his child was difficult; but he also stipulated that Claire should have £6,000, and he allocated to her a further £6,000 in words that strongly suggested she was pregnant and this extra money was to help provide for the coming infant. This bequest could be taken to imply that Shelley accepted some responsibility for her pregnancy, but when the baby was born, in January of the following year, Byron acknowledged it must almost certainly be his, the result of the sexual relations he had had with Claire back in April (even if she was then living with Shelley and Mary in what some of their more prejudiced critics assumed was a *ménage à trois*). There may sometimes have been a very slight doubt in Byron's mind about the paternity of the daughter to whom Claire gave birth, but he accepted responsibility for her willingly enough.[2]

From Saint-Gingolph, the two poets sailed on to Villeneuve at the eastern end of the lake and visited the nearby medieval castle of Chillon, which stands partly in the water. What particularly impressed them were the dungeons, with the huge pillars to which, their guide explained, prisoners were chained. The water lapping against the walls made it an especially evocative place and it prompted in Byron one of his most popular and successful poems. *The Prisoner of Chillon* describes the fate of Bonnivard, a Swiss Protestant imprisoned in Chillon by his Catholic enemies and forced to watch two of his brothers, also chained to pillars, die before him and be buried by their gaolers in shallow graves only a few feet away. The poem is good at evoking both the atmosphere of the dungeon and the psychological effect of long imprisonment on Bonnivard when he is finally released, and became well known all

The dungeons of Château de Chillon.

over Europe. From Villeneuve, Byron and Shelley sailed on along the northern shore of the lake and stopped in Vevey and Clarens, two locations which Rousseau knew very well and which figure prominently in *Julie*.

In many ways, Byron was the perfect tourist. He loved to visit places where great people had lived, or great events had taken place, and then celebrate them in verse. But in the case of Vevey and Clarens he was equally excited by locations that had provided the environment for what were only fictional characters: 'Clarens! Sweet Clarens! Birthplace of deep love!', he wrote in the third canto and, in a note to the stanza this line introduces, he quotes a passage from Rousseau's *Confessions* in which he urges his readers to visit the area around Vevey and decide for themselves whether it was not the perfect setting for the characters in *Julie*. Amplifying the thoughts in the stanza, Byron adds his own gloss to Rousseau's words by insisting that the area around these small towns, as well as 'the opposite rocks of Meillerie', are invested with something even more than the 'mere sympathy with individual passion':

> it is a sense of the existence of love in its most extended and
> sublime capacity, and of our own participation of its good
> and of its glory: it is the great principle of the universe,
> which is there more condensed, but not less manifested;
> and of which, though knowing ourselves a part, we lose our
> individuality, and mingle in the beauty of the whole. (*LB* 144)

There is another hint of Wordsworth's solipsism here, but given that love was not exactly that poet's strong suit, what the passage indicates more obviously is how strong an influence Shelley's transcendentalism was having on Byron at this time.

From Vevey they went on to Ouchy and then back to Cologny on 30 June. Byron was highly satisfied with the trip, which had given him material for *The Prisoner of Chillon* and which would also allow him to finish Canto III of *Childe Harold*. He seems to have no reservations about Shelley as a companion, whereas the younger man had developed a few about him which he would go on to express in a letter to his friend Thomas Peacock in the middle of July. Acknowledging that Byron had shown him 'great kindness', he regretted that the effect of his own company had not been enough to lessen 'those superstitions of rank & wealth & revenge & servility to opinion with which he, in common with other men, is too poisonously imbued'.[3] By contrast, when Byron was about to leave Diodati at the end of September, he urged his friend Kinnaird to 'continue to like Shelley', who was by then back in England, as 'he is a very good – very clever – but a very singular man – he was a great comfort to me here by his intelligence and good nature' (*BLJ* V.107).

When Byron first arrived in Geneva, he had a list of contacts who gave him an entrée into the town's high society, but after participating in a number of social occasions, he decided they were not for him. He seemed happy enough with the company of the Shelleys and intermittent sexual relations with Claire, but while she must have hoped that the more he got to know her the more he would like her, the opposite seems to have occurred. By August, he was refusing to sleep with Claire in what may have been a response to her pregnancy but could also have been a consequence of how aware he had become of the rumours circulating among the many expatriates that what had been established in Cologny was a commune where free love was practised.

He had received news in July that Sheridan had died. When Byron was on the management committee of Drury Lane, he had got to know him well, often accompanying the drunken old man home after a night on the town. He would remember with glee how once when Sheridan was lying dead drunk in a gutter and had been challenged by a watchman for his name, he gave him 'William Wilberforce', the famously clean-living and puritanical leader of the anti-slavery movement. The monody he wrote to commemorate Sheridan's death includes a reference to the secret enemies who spy on the famous:

Behold the host! Delighting to deprave,
Who track the steps of Glory to the grave,
Watch every fault that daring Genius owes

Half to the ardour which its birth bestows,
Distort the truth – accumulate the lie
And pile the Pyramid of Calumny! (*CPW* IV.21)

This clearly applied as much to himself as to Sheridan.

There was, however, one person in the Geneva area determined not to allow Byron to shut himself away from the world. This was Madame de Staël, who in June had returned to her family estate at Coppet, a village diagonally across the lake from Cologny. She had known Byron when she was living in England in 1813 and had been delighted when, in a note to a line in his *Bride of Abydos*, he had referred to her book on Germany as being by 'the first female writer of this, perhaps of any, age' (*CPW* III.346). Although he found her loquacity wearing, Byron admired her intelligence and felt she was essentially good-natured, so that, as she began peppering him with invitations to her salon, he eventually relented and developed a habit of sailing across the lake to join her and her many guests. He was later to say that Madame de Staël had made Coppet 'as agreeable as society and talent can make any place on earth' (*BLJ* V.109). He always spoke warmly of her, and what made his visits especially comfortable for him was her fluent English, because, although Byron could read French without difficulty, he had never learnt to speak it well. It is likely that he did not have to even try at Coppet given that the other guests included all the leading figures in the local liberal intelligentsia. There was also a sprinkling of English visitors, including a lady who is said to have fainted when Byron appeared for the first time, although whether this was from horror or excitement is not clear. Certainly, his reputation among this last group cannot have been improved by a recently published novel called *Glenarvon* which his hostess was able to pass on to him and in which Lady Caroline Lamb gave a lightly fictionalized account of her affair with him.

Polidori sometimes accompanied Byron to Coppet, but Shelley declined to do so and instead decided it was time to take Mary and

Claire to Chamonix where they could explore the area dominated by Mont Blanc. This was in late July and by the time his party came back he began preparing a return to England, where there were urgent financial matters which had to be dealt with, and where he also needed to begin making arrangements for Claire's lying in. He did not leave until the end of August, just in time to meet Hobhouse, who was finally keeping his promise to visit Byron in Switzerland so that they could continue on together into Italy. Appearing with him was Scrope Davies, that other old friend from Byron's Cambridge days, and the three of them may well have fallen into their old mocking, smoking-room idiom, which was not at all to Shelley's taste.

After the Shelley party had gone, and Davies was on his way home, Byron and Hobhouse took a trip to the Mont Blanc region. This was cut short because of the continuing bad weather but they had much better luck in September when they decided to visit the mountain range which includes the Jungfrau and the Eiger. Byron was so impressed by the scenery there that he chose it as the setting for *Manfred*, the new poetic drama he was writing (in the second scene of this work, the protagonist is contemplating a leap to his death from the Jungfrau). This was a new departure, reflective of an interest Byron had always had in the drama that had been further stimulated by his time at Drury Lane. As he quickly came to realize and accept, however, it was a play that was hardly performable, because in the first place there was too little of what might be called action and, in the second, it really consisted of only one developed character: Manfred himself.

Manfred spends much of his time calling up spirits, Faustus-like, although, in his case, from a bewildering variety of religious and mythological sources. Essentially another and more extreme version of the Byronic hero, he is haunted by the memories of inexpiable crimes committed in the past, old before his time, and weary of both the world and himself (hence the temptation of

John Martin, *Manfred on the Jungfrau*, 1837, watercolour.

suicide). The spirits who appear are often like the demons with
which a tormented individual, agonizingly conscious of his own
failings and misdeeds but too proud to accept the right of others to
pass judgement on them, heroically struggles in what is less a play
in the usual sense than a psychodrama. As it develops, *Manfred*
includes a number of phrases that Byron had already used when
writing a long and detailed account of the trip to the Bernese Alps
for Augusta. He had been communicating with his half-sister
regularly, assuring her in what are essentially love letters of how
devoted he remained, and on one occasion even saying how much
better it would have been if neither of them had married and they
could have spent their lives together. But he was disconcerted
by the relatively tepid nature of her responses. What he did not
know was that, once he had left England, Augusta had fallen
completely under the control of his wife. Having extorted from her
a confession that she had slept with Byron, Annabella set herself
the task of bringing Augusta to a full recognition of the enormity
of her crime and a repentance which would be in tune with her own

increasingly evangelical version of Christianity. The power she had lay in the fact that, if she cut off her relations with Augusta, it would be confirmation of the rumours of incest which were rife in their shared social world, and probably mean that she would have to give up her job as a lady-in-waiting. How extensive the power was can be judged by her having compelled Augusta to show her every letter Byron wrote so that when he said that neither of them should have married, Annabella was probably listening in.

Manfred is completely alienated from society; the only person he has felt close to in the past is a certain 'Lady Astarte'. Although this figure may be partly inspired by Annabella, there are strong suggestions that it was primarily based on Augusta. Manfred describes her, for example, as 'like me in lineaments – her eyes,/ Her hair, her features, to the very tone/ Even of her voice, they said were like to mine;/ But soften'd all, and temper'd into beauty'; and as the sole companion of his wanderings, she was 'the only thing he seem'd to love –/ As he, indeed, by blood was bound to' (*LB* 291–2). When later he commands his spirits to conjure her up, he says, 'it was the deadliest sin to love as we have loved.' Of this one consolation of the failed and tortured life Manfred is looking back on, he says, 'I loved her, and destroy'd her' (*LB* 300), words which, when Byron was writing this work, were probably truer than he realized at the time.

That the weather remained fine during the whole of their Alpine trip helped to make it a success. Returning to Diodati at the end of September, Byron and Hobhouse made their preparations for Italy. Rushton had gone home with Davies, and the household was further reduced by a decision that Polidori was surplus to requirements. It was partly that, while Byron had often been ill during his final months in England, the relative calm of Switzerland seems to have settled his system and meant that he had no especial need of constantly available medical treatment. But it was also that Polidori had turned out to be hot-headed, and on at least two occasions had got himself into trouble with the Genevan authorities. 'I have enough to do to manage my own scrapes,' Byron later commented (*BLJ* V.163). The two parted amicably and the long-planned journey to Italy could begin.

7

Venice

On leaving Switzerland, Hobhouse and Byron first took the Simplon
Pass into Italy and then headed for Milan, where they arrived on
12 October 1816. Their fortnight in that city was made more
interesting by a number of encounters, one of which was with a
short, corpulent individual called Henri Beyle. He had fascinating
information to impart about what it was like working for Napoleon
because he had occupied a post in the emperor's secretariat of
sufficient importance to have allowed him the dubious privilege
of participation in the Russian campaign. There is little doubt
that 'Stendhal', as Henri Beyle later became known, embroidered
his accounts a little, but that he had indeed been in Moscow with
Napoleon, and been able to observe his behaviour both there and
during the retreat, made him an intriguing figure for two men who
were always eager to know more about their fallen idol.

Leaving Milan on 3 November, the two travellers arrived in
Venice a week later. This was where Hobhouse was expecting to
meet some of his relatives so that they could then take a sightseeing trip to Rome, but Byron intended to settle for a while and
therefore took lodgings in a house not far from St Mark's Square.
His landlord, Pietro Segati, was a draper, whose young and beautiful
wife, Marianna, soon became Byron's mistress, although with the
connivance of her husband, who had his own mistress elsewhere.
Claire Clairmont had not succeeded in allowing Byron to forget the
mental torments which he believed Annabella Milbanke had caused

him, but Marianna Segati did. 'I do not think a human being ever suffered a greater degree of mental torture than I have undergone,' he wrote to his wife from Milan, 'since & during our separation' (*BLJ* V.120); but it was rare that he complained to her directly. His more usual way of relieving his feelings was in letters to Augusta in which he felt he could more freely combine accounts of what he had suffered with a previously suppressed but now growing hostility to Annabella. But he was still writing *Manfred* at this stage and was therefore able to express through its central character, if only indirectly, how troubled he felt, and yet also how defiant.

In a letter Byron wrote to Moore at the end of January 1817, he described how he had been 'half mad' during the composition of Canto III of *Childe Harold* largely on account of 'love inextinguishable, thoughts unutterable, and the nightmare of my own delinquencies', and then went on to say that he would have blown his brains out but for the pleasure his suicide would have given his mother-in-law (*BLJ* V.165). What is unusual in both Manfred and his creator is that any sense of 'delinquencies' does not lessen the fury with which they proudly resist those who would criticize or persecute them. Lady Byron's advisors were fond of hinting that, if it came to a court battle, there were 'things' they *could* say about her husband that would be devastating. What are these things? he countered, defying them to do their worst and forgetting that to be exposed as someone who had slept with his half-sister, and had several homosexual relationships, would hardly have made him seem, in the England of his time, a fit person to be involved in (for example) the education of his child. When *Manfred* was published in June 1817, one reviewer went as far as asking why we should feel sympathetic towards the protagonist when he has committed incest, 'one of the most revolting of all crimes', before adding, 'Lord Byron has coloured *Manfred* into his own personal features.'[1] Augusta turned to Annabella for advice about dealing with situations of this kind and was instructed by her to speak about *Manfred* only 'with the most decided expressions of disapprobation'. In an indication of the knowledge the two women now shared, she went on, 'He practically gives you away, and implies you were guilty *after* marriage.'[2] Byron was increasingly puzzled by the way the fervour with which he wrote to Augusta was not reciprocated; but he betrayed a lack of imaginative sympathy in failing to understand that the defiant boldness he himself was always ready to show, and with which he endows Manfred, could lead to serious collateral damage.

He had always maintained that, in spite of the anguish she had caused him, he still loved his wife; but as he settled into his new Venetian life, that conviction faded. 'At present if she would rejoin me tomorrow –', he told Augusta in February 1817, 'I would not accept the proposition' (*BLJ* V.175). He found himself becoming increasingly fond of Marianna and it suited his mood to be in a town full of historical monuments to past glory. That there were a number of local aristocrats ready to welcome his company, and few English tourists around to stare at this man whom they had all read about in their newspapers, did not make Venice less enjoyable. More mundanely, it was also a town where life was cheap. He gave a startling instance of this in describing how in January he had rented a box at the Fenice theatre. It cost him, he reported to Augusta, 'about *14* pounds sterling for the season instead of *four hundred* as in London' (*BLJ* V.160).

Since the separation, there had been a revolution in Byron's attitude to money. A clear sign of how differently he now felt about financial matters is apparent in his relations with his publisher. From being someone reluctant to accept anything at all for what he wrote, he became a tough negotiator, keen to extract as much as possible from Murray. He was aware that although he laboured hard over *Manfred*, rewriting the third act, it was a new departure and might not go down well with his public (although in fact it became one of the texts by which he was best known, especially in Europe) and therefore asked for the relatively small sum of 300 guineas. Yet at the same time he was insistent that he wanted an equivalent amount for a short poem of just under 250 lines called *The Lament of Tasso*, which he had written in a day or two.

Byron was inspired to write this poem when, after having thoroughly immersed himself in Venice's carnival celebrations, and then suffered a bout of what was becoming his recurrent fever, he finally set off in April 1817 to join Hobhouse and his relations in Rome. It was on the way there that he passed through Ferrara, a town already interesting to him as the home of the Este family and the protagonists in his poem *Parisina*. He was shown in Ferrara a room where Parisina and her lover were supposedly executed, and also the apartment in the building where Tasso had been confined for seven years. He was an especially interesting figure for Byron in that he had been designated mad by Ferrara's rulers only because, it was falsely rumoured, he had fallen in love with the Marquess of Ferrara's sister. Am I not angry with those who have had me confined? Byron's Tasso asks, 'Who have debased me in the minds of men,/ Debarring me the usage of my own'. He then declares himself 'too proud to be vindictive' (*CPW* IV.119). Sympathetic though Byron might have felt towards Tasso, his short poem had little quality and 300 guineas was a lot to ask for it. But he no doubt felt that Murray must have profited hugely from his previous work and believed it was time to be compensated a little.

More tourism and sightseeing, in Rome but also on his way to and from there, prompted Byron into continuing *Childe Harold* with a fourth and final canto. He was busy with this when, at the beginning of June, having arrived back in Venice with Hobhouse, he rented an old villa at Mira, about 11 kilometres (7 mi.) out of the city in order to avoid the summer heat. From there, on the first of July, he sent Murray the opening stanza of the new canto, saying that he had already completed thirty more and warning him that, as far as price went, 'I mean to be as mercenary as possible.'

Byron's summer retreat at Mira, from an engraving by J. F. Costa.

The most striking feature of this new poem is that Byron completely abandoned any pretence of speaking through a persona: its 'I' is openly and frankly autobiographical. A major theme which runs through is departed glory, so that, as he puts in the third stanza, 'In Venice, Tasso's echoes are no more,/ And silent rows the songless gondolier' (*LB* 149). This nostalgic note chimes in well with Byron's recurrent sense of being someone the interesting part of whose life is now behind him, so that, driven to 'meditate amongst decay', he is able to describe himself melodramatically as 'A ruin amidst ruins' (*LB* 155). As a travel writer in verse, Byron has only a mild interest in Italian art, but the buildings are like battlefields, stimulating his interest in the past. In Rome he describes at length the current state of the Palatine, the Pantheon and of course the Coliseum, that 'long explored but still exhaustless mine/ Of contemplation' (*LB* 185).

Byron demanded 2,500 guineas for the new canto instead of the 1,500 Murray initially offered, even though he must have known that it describes places which had been described many times before and did not have the exotic unfamiliarity of, for example, Albania. What always made his publisher nervous, however, were his writer's politics. In calling him a 'bastard Caesar', or accusing him of vanity, Byron is hardly kind to Napoleon in this work, but he laments again the state of Europe after Waterloo and feels that now one has to look to America for successful liberation movements. Italy is, after all, like Greece in being deprived of its freedom by reactionary powers, a fact which adds to the melancholy with which its ruins and decaying monuments, testimony to its current powerlessness, can be explored. But it was precisely this melancholy which Byron's many followers seem to have found appealing, especially when it took a personal form as it now did so directly, and without any pretence of an invented spokesman. There is a striking expression of it at the end of a section of Canto IV where, after contemplating the spring associated with the nymph Egeria, Byron is reflecting on the transience of love:

> We wither from our youth, we gasp away –
> Sick – sick; unfound the boon, unslaked the thirst,
> Though to the last, in verge of our decay,
> Some phantom lures, such as we sought at first –
> But all too late, – so are we doubly curst.
> Love, fame, ambition, avarice – 'tis the same,
> Each idle – and all ill – and none the worst –
> For all are meteors with a different name,
> And Death the sable smoke where vanishes the flame. (*LB* 183–4)

This is the *weltschmertz* which had made Goethe's *Sorrows of Young Werther* (1774) such a popular text and in Byron's case it was no doubt nourished by genuine periods of depression and despair.

And yet, as he had explained to Moore in March 1817, Byron was not always in this kind of mood – not, that is, 'a misanthropical and gloomy gentleman', or someone who, as he describes himself in Canto IV, had recourse to Nature in order to 'all forget the human race'. In fact, he was sometimes (he reminded Moore) 'a facetious companion . . . as loquacious and laughing as if I were a much cleverer fellow' (*BIJ* V.186). A public demonstration that there were two distinct sides to his nature would come when he was visited by English friends in September and shown an account, in mock-heroic verse, of certain members of King Arthur's Round Table in conflict with giants which purported to be by the brothers 'Whistlecraft'. The real author was a retired English diplomat almost twenty years older than Byron called Frere, who had managed to sustain a jaunty, cheerful mood throughout two cantos of 60 and then 56 stanzas apiece, and in an English version of the *ottava rima* (ababacc), which had been employed by certain Italian comic writers of the fifteenth century whom Byron particularly admired. He was much taken with this poem and in no time at all he had dashed off one in the same metre. His is longer than Frere's, but much better, in part because it was far more firmly grounded in contemporary realities.

Beppo, the diminutive in Italian of Giuseppe, is a version of an anecdote told to Byron by Marianna Segati's husband. It concerned a Venetian merchant who had failed to return from one of his business trips overseas, and the complications which followed, for his wife and the lover she had taken during the long period of his absence, when he suddenly and unexpectedly turned up again. What it reflects is the tolerant and distinctly un-English attitudes to sexual morality which Byron felt he had discovered in Venice, and how happy he initially was living there. Its tone is a triumph of witty and easy-going geniality, with a smattering of those comic rhymes which would become a Byron speciality: 'Verona' and 'known a', for example, or 'quote is' and 'notice'. Its narrator presents himself as a 'broken Dandy lately on [his] travels' (*LB* 329) and, as he tells his story of how his heroine dealt with the return of her long-lost husband, he is full of digressions. Most of these are about how relaxed and pleasant relations in Venice are, especially relations between the sexes, and why he prefers to live there rather than in England. With his tongue firmly in his cheek, he claims that it is largely a question of climate ('To see the Sun set, sure he'll rise tomorrow') and also of the Italian cuisine, although he does point out that, during Lent, Venetians tend to eat their fish without sauce so any Englishman needs to come well equipped with 'Ketchup, Soy, Chilli-vinegar, and Harvey/ Or, by the Lord! a Lent will well nigh starve ye' (*LB* 327, 318).

When the heroine of the poem, Laura, goes to a masked ball at Carnival time, she finds herself being stared at by a man who, in dress and complexion, seems to be a Turk. Familiar as she is with being looked at closely by men, this 'one person seemed to stare/ With pertinacity that's rather rare'. Returning home at dawn with her lover, she finds herself confronted by this same person, who reveals himself as her husband and explains how he was captured by pirates and sold into slavery before becoming a pirate himself. Prospering in that trade, he has now made his way home to reclaim all that belonged to his former life. Confrontations such as this have the potential for both tragedy and comedy, but the mood established from the beginning of *Beppo* makes it clear that we are not here in the world of the Othello who, as the narrator has already observed, was ready 'To suffocate a wife no more than twenty/ Because she had a *cavalier servente*' (*LB* 320). The familiar comedy of embarrassment is the worst that English readers can expect at this point, although, in fact, the joke turns out to be on them as they witness how quickly and easily all three participants in the action adapt to their new circumstances. Initially wrong-footed by her husband's unexpected reappearance, Laura reasserts herself with a rapid series of questions and her own version of 'what kept you?' ('And how came you to keep away so long/ Are you not sensible 'twas very wrong?'; *LB* 339). As the husband adapts to Western life once again and disposes of his Turkish clothing, the lover helps out by lending him some of his own underwear, and we are told that afterwards the two were 'always friends'.

The general message of *Beppo* is live-and-let-live, with a particular suggestion to English readers that they ought to think about taking a more relaxed attitude to life in general, and sex in particular. Nothing could be more different from the manner of *Beppo* than the one Byron had adopted in Canto IV of *Childe Harold*, which he was writing during roughly the same period, so that what it illustrates well is how he could be melodramatically involved in the story of his own sufferings and misdeeds but then also the 'facetious companion' he described himself as in his letter to Moore. For the moment, he took what he imagined would be the world's valuation of these two aspects, telling Murray that he was happy to include *Beppo* in the deal over *Childe Harold* at no extra cost. With the advantage of hindsight, it may seem that, as far as enduring *literary* value goes, those terms might just as well have been reversed.

With his interest in money sharpened, it was not too blunted by news from England at the end of 1817 that Hanson had at last managed to find a buyer for Newstead. Given that Byron was ready to let the estate go cheaply if only he could dispose of it, the price of £94,500 seems reasonable, especially if one takes into account the £25,000 the previous buyer had been obliged to forfeit when he found he could not complete the purchase. The details of the sale would take another year to work out and it was not as though Byron had sudden and ready access to such a huge sum: a third was needed to help clear his debts, with the rest going into a trust for his wife, although he then had a right to the resulting interest. But the maintenance of the original marriage agreement meant that he could look forward to more money once his mother-in-law had died, and he still had the eventual sale of Rochdale to rely on so that, from this date onwards, his financial worries weakened considerably.

In January 1818, Hobhouse left for England, carrying with him the manuscript of Canto IV of *Childe Harold* to give to Murray. The departure of his somewhat stolid friend from Greece in 1810 had been the signal for a period of dissipation and something similar appears to have happened now, although all the evidence available suggests that Byron's increased sexual activity was exclusively with women, which had not been the case before. 'I will work the mine of my youth to the last veins of the ore, and then – good night. I have lived, am content,' he told Tom Moore (*BLJ* VI.10–11). His affair with Marianna Segati had come to an end and in May 1818 he rented the Palazzo Mocenigo on the Grand Canal where, looked after by fourteen servants, he could entertain as many women as he liked: later he would claim to have slept with over two hundred, and his letters sometimes give the impression that fornication was his chief pastime in this period. That cannot, however, have been entirely true; having had some horses brought to the Lido at Venice, he was able to ride there regularly, and he also spent a good deal of time swimming, often with a former veteran of the Napoleonic army called Mengaldo. This man was given to boasting about how he had once swum across the Beresina under enemy fire, so it gave Byron satisfaction to establish that he had much less staying power in the water than himself.

Palazzo Mocenigo on the Grand Canal in Venice.

The life Byron was living at this time shocked the few English friends who visited him and they claimed that it had led to a physical deterioration in the handsome young poet they had previously known. His own awareness that he was putting on weight again (his perennial problem), along with the beginnings of grey hair, only made him feel that he ought to make the best of the short time he had left. In the meantime, quite a lot of it must have been spent in writing. It was in this period, for example, that he wrote *Mazeppa*, a strange tale supposedly told to Charles XII of Sweden after the Battle of Poltava by the famous Cossack leader of the title. He describes how, when he was a page at the Polish court, an affair he was having with one of its ladies was discovered and the outraged husband strapped him naked to a horse which was then set running off into the countryside until it dropped from exhaustion. Released by local peasants from the dead animal, Mazeppa is nursed back to life by them and eventually recovers sufficiently to become a famous warrior and take his revenge. These semi-legendary events may have caught Byron's interest because he was doing so much horse-riding at the time (the mad gallop of Mazeppa's horse through wild terrain is remarkably well described), but its narrative is managed as expertly as in any of those 'Eastern tales' which had solidified his fame.

More or less contemporary with *Mazeppa* is Byron's 'Ode to Venice', another lament over departed Venetian glories, the grim tone of which has a lot in common with the final canto of *Childe Harold*. It was reading this canto which caused Shelley's friend Peacock to say that one ought to 'take a stand against the encroachments of black bile'.[3] He probably did not then know that Byron himself, having already provided one counter to the gloomier aspect of his nature in *Beppo*, was now following that up with the extraordinary achievement of the first two cantos of *Don Juan*.

Prompted by what must have been at least his own sense of its success, he adopted for this new venture the same tolerant, witty and worldly wise narrative voice he had developed in *Beppo*, and the same verse form. He chose Cádiz as its opening setting and teased his readers' expectations by imagining his hero as first of all a naive, innocent adolescent whose sexual adventures are more a matter of accident than design. His mother has a friend called Donna Julia who is married to a man much older than herself, and Juan is with her in bed when the husband comes knocking at the door. The resulting episodes, with the husband unsuccessfully searching the room, his wife and her maid hiding Juan between them in the bed, Donna Julia's mock outrage at the intrusion ('Ungrateful, perjured, barbarous Don Alfonso,/ How dare you think your lady would go on so?'; *LB* 414), and the eventual discovery of Juan's shoes, have all the ingredients of sophisticated bedroom farce and Byron handles them with admirable skill, wit and aplomb. But when Hobhouse and his other friends in England read the poem, they concurred in thinking it should not be published, a judgement which at first Byron accepted but then fortunately decided he wanted to ignore.

The reason for his friends' disapproval was perhaps the light and comic fashion in which the first canto of *Don Juan* dealt with adultery (and the second with extramarital sex); but they mainly seem to have been made nervous by a recognizable portrait of Lady Byron with which Juan's story more or less begins. She is cast as the boy's mother, Donna Inez, a highly educated woman whose 'favourite science was the mathematical' and whose worst faults are that she hasn't got any. 'But – Oh! ye lords of ladies intellectual', Byron writes in a famous rhyme, 'Inform us truly, have they not hen-peck'd you all?' (*LB* 383). His account of Donna Inez's troubled relationship with her husband recalls details of his separation from his own wife:

Richard Westall, illustration for *Don Juan* (1820), canto I, stanza 170.

> For Inez call'd some druggists and physicians,
>   And tried to prove her loving lord was *mad*,
> But as he had some lucid intermissions,
>   She next decided he was only *bad*; (*LB* 384)

The tone throughout is genial, much more Horatian than Juvenalian, one might say, although with an undercurrent of bitterness; and it is maintained as Byron goes on to describe the difficulties Donna Inez encounters as she supervises Juan's education in the classics, chiefly because of the way the far from respectable behaviour of the deities, male and female, is sometimes described in classical texts.

How best to bring up children was a question that must often have been in Byron's mind at this period, as he wondered how his daughter would be educated, and whether she would be taught to disapprove of her father, if not positively hate him. His powerlessness to intervene in what happened to Ada may have had some influence on his attitude to the baby girl over whose bringing up he did have control since he had agreed to pay for it. After he had left Geneva and returned to England, Shelley had arranged for Claire Clairmont to give birth away from anyone they knew so that even her parents were not aware of what was happening. Claire and a daughter (called Allegra, at Byron's specific request) then came to live with Shelley and Mary until, in the wake of numerous legal and financial difficulties, Shelley decided to profit from Allegra being just about old enough to be transferred to Byron's care and travel to Italy with her, Mary and Claire on the expectation of settling in that country permanently. They initially found a house in the Milan area while Allegra was dispatched to her father in the company of a nursemaid, since Byron had made it very clear that, although he was willing to take responsibility for the child, he wanted nothing more to do with her mother.

The situation was a difficult one for Shelley. Claire had once been his lover and he remained close to her – too close, her half-sister Mary seems sometimes to have felt; but he must have been aware how much Byron resented any attempt to use Allegra in order to reignite a relationship that had largely been of Claire's making in the first place, and in which Byron now had no interest. And yet how could one separate a child from its mother? He pleaded his sister-in-law's case as best he could, yet, when he went to see Byron in Venice in August 1818, he hid from him that he had brought Claire with him. Allegra herself had delighted her father when he first met her in May, and he reported in his letters how much enthusiasm she aroused in the people he knew in Venice; but he was aware that the succession of mistresses passing through the Palazzo Mocenigo hardly made it a suitable environment for a child and he soon entrusted her care to a couple who had become his friends: Richard Hoppner, the British consul in Venice, and his Swiss wife. It was from Hoppner that Byron had rented a villa in the outskirts of the city which he intended to use as another summer retreat but was currently empty. Not knowing that Claire was already with him, Byron invited Shelley to use this property for bringing her to Venice so that she could be with her daughter. This meant that Mary could also come to the borrowed house while the two men spent time with each other in the city and rediscovered the good relationship they had established in Geneva.

Byron always enjoyed the company of Shelley, who testified in a poem describing their conversations together in Venice, *Julian and Maddalo*, that his friend was 'gentle, patient and unassuming', as well as 'cheerful, frank and witty'. But he also thought Byron was a person of consummate genius and greatly admired most of what he wrote, including *Don Juan*. This was important to Byron because the British critics were no less disapproving of its second canto than the first (with its supposed portrait of his wife). After his escapade with Donna Julia, the poem's young hero is packed off by his mother on a grand tour, accompanied by a tutor called Pedrillo, but is then shipwrecked in or near the Gulf of Lions. The harrowing details of this episode are described with a vividness and knowledgeable precision worthy of a poet whose grandfather had published a well-known account of his own shipwreck; but the tone Byron adopts makes this canto one of the most striking examples of dark humour in English literature. Along with Juan and Pedrillo, a number of sailors manage to escape the sinking ship in a long boat. Threatened with starvation, they draw lots to see who should be eaten first. The choice falls on Juan's tutor, the inedible parts of whom are thrown overboard so that they 'Regaled two sharks, who follow'd o-er the billow' while 'The sailors ate the rest of poor Pedrillo' (*LB* 452). Touches of this kind – or the more obvious, cruder one in which the long boat's occupants, having looked with appreciation at the 'master's mate' as the fattest individual on offer, reject him when he explains that he is suffering from a disease he has caught in Cádiz, 'By general subscription of the ladies' (*LB* 453) – did not please everyone and Byron was widely accused of cynicism and heartlessness. Yet although in his account of the shipwreck Byron is often sardonic, it is usually only in recognition of how most human beings will tend to behave in extreme circumstances. He no more gloats over the sufferings of the shipwrecked sailors than, in the succeeding episodes – after Juan, the eventual sole survivor of the wreck, is washed up on an island ruled by a wealthy pirate and then brought back to life by this man's young daughter – he devalues the charming description of the love which develops between these two naive adolescents with an occasional witty aside. In what became a very long poem, there are bound to be misjudgements of tone, but what one can say of such a multifaceted phenomenon as Byron's sense of humour is that, in general, it enables him to enclose both love and suffering within his comic world without making either seem ridiculous or suggest that he was, in himself, peculiarly hard-hearted.

When Byron's compatriots found elements that they disapproved of in his writing, they tended to link them to his profligate way of life. Of the excessive gloom in Canto IV of *Childe Harold*, for example, even Shelley claimed that it could be traced back to its author's association with Italian women, than whom 'no human beings could be more contemptible'. Even Italian countesses, he wrote, 'smell so of garlick that an ordinary Englishman cannot approach them'.[4] Whether or not she smelt of garlic, it was an Italian countess who brought Byron out of what had been more than a year of exceptionally loose living. He had first seen Teresa Guiccioli in January 1818 when she was eighteen years old and the very recent third wife of an Italian count almost three times her own age; but it was only in the summer of the following year when Byron met her again, at an aristocratic gathering, that he fell desperately in love with her, as she with him. Teresa's husband was not Venetian but from Ravenna, and when he decided to take Teresa back there, and she urged her lover to follow her, Byron felt he could do nothing but comply.

8

Ravenna Twice Over

As much in love with Teresa as he had been as an adolescent with Mary Chaworth, Byron could nevertheless never quite get rid of a nagging feeling, as he followed her to Ravenna, Bologna, Venice again and then back to Ravenna, that he was wasting his life in devoting himself to a woman in this way. Although he kept on writing wherever he happened to settle, being now recognized as a famous poet all over Europe was not enough to make him feel he was living an entirely worthwhile life. It was in Ravenna that Dante was buried, having lived his last days in exile there, and because Byron's visit to Ferrara had produced his *Lament of Tasso,* he was urged by Teresa to celebrate Italy's greatest poet in some way while in the city. The result was *The Prophecy of Dante,* four short cantos in which Byron attempted (not very successfully) to produce an English version of the terza rima in which *The Divine Comedy* had been written. This poem features Dante shortly before his death, foretelling how often Italy would be invaded in the future and suggesting (in Canto II) that the only remedy would be unification. It hung fire for several months, and gains some of its effect from Byron's identification with Dante as an exile, 'Ripp'd from all kindred, from all home' (*CPW* IV.221), but a major emphasis is on the unhappy fate of poets in their relation to political power so that, in the end, one might infer that this is what Byron had come to suspect mattered most.

As a hereditary member of the House of Lords, Byron had enjoyed a head start in his boyhood ambition of becoming a

Dante's tomb in Ravenna.

political leader; but he soon gave up the idea. His friend Hobhouse, on the other hand, on his return to Britain, had made a first, unsuccessful attempt at being elected as an MP for Westminster and allied himself with some of the more radical members of the Whig opposition. It was a time of considerable social unrest in Britain, especially before and after more than a dozen people attending a reform meeting in Manchester's St Peter's Field were killed by the authorities in an episode which became ironically known as 'Peterloo'. The Tories had been introducing what was even for them unusually repressive legislation and were struggling to bring the public finances into order in the wake of the indebtedness brought about by the Napoleonic Wars. A rumour that alarmed Byron was that the government, in order to balance the books, wanted to arbitrarily seize 25 per cent of the assets of all those holding

William Edward West, *George Gordon, 6th Lord Byron, 1788–1824. Poet*, 1822, oil on canvas.

government bonds. Since Byron was now one of these, he swore he would return to England in order to take up arms against any such measure; and his fighting talk increased as his friends began to suggest that matters were reaching such a pass that there was every prospect of a revolution.

Had there in fact been a revolution in England at this time, one has to wonder: which side would Byron have found himself fighting on? In a letter to Augusta in October 1819, he admitted, 'I am not democrat enough to like the tyranny of blackguards – such fellows as Bristol Hunt are a choice of evils with Castlereagh – except that a gentleman scoundrel is always preferable to a vulgar one' (*BLJ* VI.229). It was of course when Hunt, who had already made a name for himself during elections in Bristol, was scheduled to address the meeting in Manchester that 'Peterloo' took place. It is impossible to imagine Byron fighting shoulder to shoulder with Castlereagh, whom he hated, but he had not felt comfortable with the middle- or lower-class radicals his liaison with Lady Oxford had led him to meet. After Hobhouse had succeeded in becoming an MP at his second attempt, partly with the support of radical groups, Byron reiterated his suspicion of the non-aristocratic left-wing in British politics, saying in February 1820 that 'If we must have a tyrant – let him at least be a gentleman who has been bred to the business, and let us fall by the axe and not the butcher's cleaver' (*BLJ* VII.44).

Revolution in England was, however, far from his thoughts as he hovered around Teresa in Ravenna, writing her love letters in Italian as passionate as any he had ever composed. In his first weeks there he was made uneasy by her illness (she was recuperating from a miscarriage) and claimed that he would poison himself should she not recover; but soon he was accompanying her to the opera, visiting her at home and riding with her in the countryside. In all of this he was baffled by the attitude of Teresa's husband, who gave every indication of buying into the fiction that the relation of his young wife to her widely recognized English *amico* was entirely platonic. This may have been because he felt Byron could be useful to him in various ways: as the source of a loan, for example, or as someone who could secure for him an unpaid post of British consul in Ravenna, which would provide insurance against future political difficulties. A cultivated, intelligent man, the last thing Count Guiccioli was as a husband was naive, so Byron was never quite free of the suspicion that he might find himself walking down a dark street one evening and have an assassin's knife planted in his back.

Henry Thomas Ryall, after William Brockedon, *Teresa Guiccioli*, 1836, stipple engraving.

It may, nonetheless, have been because the relationship between Byron and Teresa was becoming too much of an open scandal that the count moved from Ravenna to one of his properties in Bologna. But Byron duly followed the couple there so that he could keep on seeing the countess (in telling Douglas Kinnaird that she was 'a sort of an Italian Caroline Lamb, except that She is much prettier, and not so savage', one of the character traits he may also have had in mind was how heedless she could be of public opinion; *BLJ* VI.135). Somehow, she managed to convince her husband that, as she was still not well, she had to go to Venice to see a well-known doctor and that, because he himself had business affairs elsewhere, Byron ought to chaperon her. What had clearly helped to make their relationship so exciting for both is that it needed to be conducted in semi-secrecy, but now they could wend their leisurely way to the villa in Mira, which Byron had chosen to retain, and for a short time live happily there together as a couple.

It was to Mira that Byron was able to invite Tom Moore, who was on his travels, and entrust to him a prose memoir of his early life with instructions that it was not to be published while its author was still alive. Since this work included an account of his marriage and separation, he would later invite Lady Byron to read it, but without success. Meanwhile he had been continuing with *Don Juan*, if somewhat hesitantly given his uncertainty about its reception, especially among his friends. Canto III, which he had completed by the time he saw Moore, is much shorter than the first two. It begins with reflections on the incompatibility between love and marriage – 'Think you, if Laura had been Petrarch's wife,/ He would have written sonnets all his life?' (*LB* 489) – and then warns the 'chaste reader' to stop reading the story of Juan and the pirate's daughter, Haidée, given how dangerous it is to hear about unmarried love. After this dig at his more puritanical critics, he moves on to a fine description, and character sketch, of Haidée's father, Lambro, as he makes his way home after another of his piratical ventures. There has been a false rumour of his death, and so, as he draws near his estate, he finds an elaborate celebration in progress which Haidée has organized for Juan's benefit (and on the assumption that she is already the inheritor of her father's wealth). Byron excels himself in his descriptions of the oriental luxury of this event, with exotic foods everywhere available and both the hostess and her lover beautifully dressed. But he is also excellent on the comedy of the homecoming of Lambro as he tries to discover what is going on by questioning a guest who fails to recognize him as both Haidée's father and the person only too painfully aware that he will be footing the bill for all the food and drink he sees around him. It is at this point that Byron abruptly decides to end the canto, leaving his reader in suspense as to what will happen once Lambro reveals who he is and reasserts his parental authority.

Count Guiccioli must have experienced a surprise a little like Lambro's when he arrived in Venice and became aware of what had been going on between his young wife and her English lover. He decided that their brief idyll should be brought to an end and drew up a long list of severe instructions as to how Teresa ought to behave in the future, which of course included not seeing any more of Byron. These were indignantly rejected by his wife, who showed no enthusiasm for going back home with her husband, clearly preferring a definitive break. But with his decade-long advantage of age and experience, Byron was aware of how difficult leaving one's husband could be for a woman, in terms of finance, reputation and future prospects, and felt that they should part, claiming that doing so would be just as painful for him as it clearly would be for her but that it was in her best interests he should make this sacrifice. Suspecting that his staying in Italy after a separation might mean the situation became more painful for Teresa, making it seem more likely that she had been 'planted' (in the then current term for what we might now call dumped), he decided that he would return to England for a while and began making all the preparations for doing so.

His plan was to take a closer look at his finances in England, and decide there what to do about Allegra. She had been cared for by a number of different people in Italy and at one point was in Bologna with her father; but she clearly needed a more settled life, particularly when it came to her education (he may well have hoped that Augusta could be persuaded to lend a hand). Staying in England for long was not in his mind, but rather that he should move on to find a quite different life elsewhere. This was the period when Simón Bolívar was liberating huge swathes of South America from Spanish control and Byron was attracted to the idea of acquiring a large property in Venezuela to begin a wholly new life there. But all these plans came to nothing when Allegra fell ill, as did the rebellious Teresa, who was showing no inclination to resume the role of a dutiful wife. So ill was Teresa that her father, having (he claimed) spoken to Count Guiccioli, took the unusual step of writing to Byron himself and urged him to return to Ravenna.

Although he seems to have been a largely willing victim, Byron's return to Ravenna at the beginning of 1820 was in some sense Teresa's victory over him, as well as over her husband. In *Beppo* he had joked that the role of *cavalier servente* was no sinecure (*LB* 326), and now he noted that it meant a man actually became 'a piece of female property' (*BLJ* VII.28). In the February following his return, he wrote a long letter to Murray in which he described his position in some detail, pointing out that it involved 'a kind of discipline' which admitted of few deviations. Italian women, he went on, are 'extremely tenacious – and jealous as furies – not permitting their lovers even to marry if they can help it . . . The reason is that they marry for their parents and love for themselves. – They exact fidelity from a lover as a debt of honour' (*BLJ* VII.43). It was a debt that Byron appears to have fully paid, continuing to justify the claim he had made in the previous year that, as far as sexual relations were concerned, he was now confining himself to the 'strictest adultery' (*BLJ* VI.232).

Life could not have been particularly easy for him in those first few days or months of 1820 given the subterfuges he and Teresa had to employ to see each other in private and the disruption entailed in moving between towns when he had a bevy of servants, horses he was always keen to have with him for exercise, and a menagerie of animals: 'two Cats – six dogs – a badger – a falcon – , a tame Crow – and a Monkey' (*BLJ* VII.209). And then there were the two nursemaids he had decided he needed to attend to Allegra. Hotels were hardly suitable locations for all these dependants, but he had difficulty finding a large property to rent in the Ravenna district. It was as early as February that Teresa's always baffling husband came to Byron's rescue by suggesting he rent the top floor of his own palazzo. He could hardly have believed that this English lord's relations with his wife were now innocent, so his motives in making this offer remain obscure, especially as moving into Teresa's own building clearly made it easier for Byron to continue having sex with her.

Signs of the degree of Byron's immersion in Italian culture at this point in his life are the Dante poem, which he finally sent off to Murray in March, and his translation of the first canto of the *Morgante* by the fifteenth-century Italian poet Luigi Pulci. This comic epic tells the story of a giant who is converted to Christianity by Orlando, one of Charlemagne's paladins, and then participates in his adventures (it is the giant who gives the work its title). It is easy to see from the translation how the poem had influenced the work by the supposed Whistlecraft brothers and then *Beppo*, although for an English reader it is not as entertaining as either; yet Byron was proud of it, and particularly of the accuracy of his rendering.

He was less pleased by his continuation of *Don Juan*, feeling that his writing was becoming dull, especially in his descriptions of how his hero was sold into slavery by Lambro and then, having been disguised as a girl, joins a harem because a sultan's favourite wife has spotted and taken a fancy to him. Yet the dullness Byron supposed or feared is hardly apparent now, especially when, after a moving description of Haidée's death in Canto IV, he describes in Canto V how Juan responds to the favourite wife's advances like Joseph does to the wife of Potiphar, before the sudden arrival of the sultan himself saves him from an awkward situation. Here the narrative skill Byron had always possessed is on full display, along with his trademark humour. Unusually for him, he claimed that he had been deprived of a certain amount of enthusiasm and verve in writing these further three cantos of *Don Juan* by the hostile reception the first two had received in some quarters. What may not have helped his mood is that when Teresa read those first two in a French translation, she was so shocked by their tone that she extorted from Byron a promise that he would not carry on with the poem without her permission.

One of the more virulent of the public attacks on the first two cantos had appeared in *Blackwood's*, a Tory magazine based in Edinburgh. What *Don Juan* illustrated, its reviewer claimed, was 'a more thorough infusion of genius and vice – power and profligacy' than could be found in any previous English poem, and that, within it, wickedness was 'inextricably mingled' with beauty and grace so that it remained 'to all ages a perpetual monument of the exalted intellect, and the depraved heart'. This was to mingle praise with blame, but the praise disappeared when the reviewer came to consider what he assumed was Byron's treatment of his wife. 'To desert her was unmanly,' he wrote, but then to 'wound her widowed privacy with unhallowed strains of cold-blooded mockery', in the figure of Donna Inez, 'was brutally, fiendishly, inexpiably mean'.[1]

In deciding to draft a reply, Byron might have limited himself to observing how this suggestion that he had left his wife, when she had left him, shows how little the reviewer really knew, but instead he insisted that he could see no resemblance between Donna Inez and Lady Byron, then adding (rather more accurately), 'my figures are not portraits.' On the separation itself, he fell back again, as he had done many times before, on the way Lady Byron's 'legal advisors' had made him suffer 'the atrocities of public rumour' without bringing any specific charges which would have allowed him to justify himself. But from defending himself in this familiar way, the belief that Southey had been one of those spreading rumours about him leads Byron into discussing the 'present deplorable state of English poetry'. Noting that, with their switch from denouncing the Tories into enjoying their patronage, Southey and Wordsworth were 'parricides of their own Principles' and hardly therefore in a position to criticize others for their morality, Byron attacks the Lake poets for having initiated a revolution in the way poetry was written which then led to a widespread lowering of standards. Much earlier, he had already told Murray that he thought 'Romantic' poets like himself were 'upon a wrong revolutionary poetical system' (*BLJ* V.265), but now he repeated and strengthened that view.

A major focus for him was the way Romanticism had often sought to establish itself by attacking Alexander Pope, who was, Byron had now decided, 'the most perfect and harmonious of poets'. Although he is aware that he had himself often in the past 'shamefully deviated' from the principles Pope represents, he insists that he has 'ever loved Pope's poetry with [his] whole soul' and says he hopes to do so until his dying day. Recalling how Dr Johnson had said that, as far as *Paradise Lost* was concerned, he could not prevail upon himself to wish 'that Milton had been a rhymer', Byron wonders whether even that great poem might not have been better, if not in heroic couplets, then in something akin to the verse forms Tasso or Dante had adopted. These are among the poets Byron then invokes to contest the idea Wordsworth had expressed in the preface to the 1815 edition of his poems that no great poet had ever enjoyed fame in his own lifetime. Giving examples of those he believed had, Byron nevertheless insists that he regards his own success as temporary. In his preface to *Peter Bell* (1819), Wordsworth talked of having worked on that poem for a long period in order to 'fit it for filling permanently a station, however humble, in the Literature of my Country'. Missing out 'however humble', Byron quotes this phrase and insists that he has no such expectations for his own work.[2]

The continuation of the private rather than public aspect of Byron and Teresa's relationship depended a good deal on the loyalty of servants, but Count Guiccioli also had his household spies. It may be thanks to one of these that in May he was able to surprise his wife and lover in a compromising situation (having previously broken into Teresa's writing desk and read some of Byron's letters to her). There was then an almighty row, with the count once again insisting that his wife should give up Byron and the countess attempting to persuade her father that he must apply to the papal authorities for a legal separation. One of the reasons Byron got on well with Teresa was that her family, the Gambas, was staunchly liberal, and he developed a particularly close and warm relationship with her slightly younger brother Pietro. Yet their political principles do not seem to have prevented them from having influence in the papal courts and, when a separation was granted, it included a quite generous monthly income for Teresa as long as she lived a respectable life back in her father's household. This removal to a family home at Filetto, about 24 kilometres (15 mi.) out of Ravenna, did not make meetings with Byron any easier, but the two lovers seem to have managed well enough and, in any event, it was not long before Teresa was able to come back to Ravenna and live with her father in his town house, where Byron could see her virtually every evening.

The liberalism of the Gambas became more significant as the political temperature rose, not only in Italy but all over Europe.

The attempt that had been made at the Congress of Vienna in 1815 to turn back the clock had come under increasing pressure and in 1820 there were calls in several European countries for constitutional reform. The Spanish monarchy was the first to have to accede to these, but in July there was a revolt in Naples which managed to extort the promise of a constitution from its king. This gave great encouragement to the numerous secret societies all over Italy that were continually plotting to obtain similar reforms from their rulers. Ravenna was part of a Papal State called the Romagna and had its own secret societies, or Carbonari as they were known. Chiefly through his increasing friendship with Pietro Gamba, Byron had enrolled in one of these groups and was prepared to fight for what Naples had achieved, or – what seemed increasingly more likely – against the soldiers the Austrians were expected to send to re-establish the status quo.

When, about this time, Allegra showed signs of being spoilt and Byron decided she should be sent to a local convent school, one of the additional reasons he gave was that she would then be 'out of harm's way' (*BLJ* VIII.97) should he find himself fighting with the Carbonari in a revolution. With German and Russian encouragement, the Austrians had assembled an army, which had begun its march on Naples in February 1821. There had been proposals for an uprising of the Carbonari in September of the previous year which had come to nothing; but now it seemed essential that, as the Austrians made their way south, there should be some resistance. But it was the speed with which the Neapolitans collapsed that, to Byron's disgust, ruined the chances of a general uprising. He was by this time knee-deep in what the authorities would rightly regard as treason against the State, having even found himself, at one critical moment, hiding a stash of weapons in his own lodgings. With spies around every corner, his involvement must have been well known, but it was not an easy matter to move against an English lord with an international reputation, and someone who had also made himself popular around Ravenna with his numerous charitable activities. But they perhaps calculated that by exiling the Gambas, along with many other of Byron's friends whom they knew to have been implicated in Carbonari activities, they would also get rid of him. If that was in fact their conscious policy, it would prove successful, although they were no doubt anxious to punish the Gambas whatever the likely consequences.

Amid all this political unrest, Byron had begun writing three works which were consistent with his growing literary conservatism. The first of these was a play, *Marino Faliero*, about a fourteenth-century Doge who was executed for conspiring against the Venetian state, and the subject of the third (*The Two Foscari*) is another Doge from the same period forced to sit in judgement on a son who prefers death to exile from Venice. Between the two, Byron was also writing a play about the seventh-century BC Assyrian king Sardanapalus, who has gone down in legend as an epitome of sensual indulgence, the voluptuary par excellence, although anyone who only came to know this figure from Delacroix's famous depiction of his death, where he is lounging on a divan surrounded by naked females, would be disappointed by Byron's version. At the beginning of the play, there are references to his 'sensual sloth', and hints of bisexuality, but he turns out to be a monarch who has deliberately turned his back on the life of war and conquest adopted by his ancestors, and simply wants his subjects to live in peace and enjoy themselves when they can. Because this tolerant attitude, and refusal to tread the paths of glory, is not what is expected of Assyrian monarchs, it precipitates rebellion. Although he struggles heroically against the rebels, his efforts only delay the inevitable and the final act finds him building a funeral pyre in his throne room and preparing bravely for self-immolation. Far from being surrounded by women at this moment, naked or otherwise, he tries to send everyone else away so that he will be the only victim; but his faithful concubine Myrrha insists on committing

Eugène Delacroix, *Death of Sardanapalus*, 1827, oil on canvas.

suicide with him. She seems to have owed her presence in the play
to Teresa, who had persuaded Byron that a love interest was an
essential element, as long as it was in the idealized form Myrrha
represents. This character was therefore an additional reason
why the opportunity that the subject of Sardanapalus offered for
exploring the appeal and dangers of dissolute living, a topic on
which Byron was a considerable expert, is ignored, and his play
became all the duller as a result.

Byron was perfectly aware that these three works were all
'closet dramas' and fundamentally undramatic; but he was proud
of them as more in tune with Greek, 'classical' notions of what
a play should be than those to be found on the current English
stage, dominated as it was by the influence of Shakespeare, whom
he would describe as 'the *worst* of models, although the most
extraordinary of writers' (*BLJ* VIII.152). When he began writing
them, his closest friends in England, the ones who had advised

against publishing *Don Juan*, approved. But as he insisted on producing more, they seem to have become less enthusiastic and he was disheartened when William Gifford, his publisher's chief advisor and a poet whom he regarded as more qualified than anyone for maintaining the standards Pope had set for satire in verse, gave them the thumbs down (*BLJ* VII.167).

Since the Gambas could no longer stay in Ravenna, the question of where they would go to live next became important for Byron, who had every intention of following them. The temporary solution was Florence, although there was talk of escaping the Italian orbit completely and settling in Switzerland. But then Byron began to remember the cold shoulder he felt he had received from a number of British tourists or residents in the Geneva area and turned against this idea. What helped him to promote an alternative scheme was a crucial visit from Shelley in August 1821.

Shelley had partly come to visit Allegra in her convent school. Having previously endorsed, along with Mary and in spite of all Claire Clairmont's vehement protests, Byron's decision to send her there, he must have felt under considerable pressure to see how the little girl – who was, after all, only four – was faring. With a largely positive report to take back to her mother, Shelley then spent several days in conversation with Byron on what must have been a whole array of topics. As the recent author of *The Cenci*, and a much better classical scholar than Byron, drama was no doubt on Shelley's agenda, along with the current political and literary scene in England, as far as these two exiles could judge it. Both of them had aspirations to exert some influence through the launching of a journal and, in Shelley's mind, this was associated with wanting Byron to help the impoverished Leigh Hunt, who, with his brother John, was associated with a liberal weekly newspaper called *The Examiner*. Co-operation on this scheme would depend on the two men being closer together and there was an opportunity for this to happen when Byron asked Shelley to help him persuade the

Thomas Charles Wageman, *Leigh Hunt*, 1815, graphite on paper.

Gambas that going to Switzerland would not be a good idea. In fact, when he left Ravenna, Shelley went to see the Gambas, who were now in Florence, and persuaded them that a good place for them to settle would be Pisa, where he and Mary were already established; and he then not only found a large house for them but one also for Byron so that he could look forward to many future hours of literary and political discussion of the kind both of them had so clearly enjoyed in Ravenna.

One of their familiar subjects must have been Wordsworth ('Turdsworth', as Byron now insisted on calling him). His recent publication of *Peter Bell* had provoked considerable mockery in liberal circles, and there had been a clever parody by a writer called Reynolds before Shelley wrote his own *Peter Bell, the Third*. This excellent poem is not without its appreciation of a Wordsworth who had once been a great poet but whose writing had now, Shelley believed, sadly deteriorated, along with his political views. When Byron followed Shelley into writing parody, there were no such concessions, because his target was Robert Southey, for whom any previous respect had by now completely evaporated. In 1819 the old king had finally died and the Prince Regent became George IV. Some formal recognition of this change was no doubt expected from the poet laureate and in 1821 Southey published a commemorative poem called *A Vision of Judgement*. After a nauseously sycophantic dedication to the new king, this has a preface in which Southey digresses into an assault on recent publications that he felt had besmirched the 'moral purity' by which English literature had, in his view, been distinguished for the previous fifty years. Claiming that 'the publication of a lascivious book is one of the worst offences which can be committed against the well-being of society,' and that 'the greater the talents of the offender, the greater is his guilt,' he calls on the government to act against these 'men of diseased hearts and depraved imaginations'. Everything in the context of his remarks indicates that Byron is the author he principally has in mind, someone who with 'a Satanic spirit of pride and audacious impiety' is the leader of what Southey terms the 'Satanic school'.[3] In some ways, this implied link between Byron and Satan is more accurate than Southey is likely to have known when he suggested it.

After his three closet dramas on historical subjects, Byron had written a rather different one. As he several times says himself, it was more like *Manfred* and 'metaphysical' in character. What he did was dramatize the story in Genesis of Cain and Abel, the main action centring around the first of these figures, who gives his name to the play. One of the attractions for Byron of this biblical story appears to have been the way it showed how the world's first family, once expelled from Paradise, had to re-establish itself by means that were necessarily incestuous. What he therefore takes care to emphasize is the deep love that exists between Cain and his sister Adah, who is the mother of their child, Enoch, and who is determined to accompany him when, after Abel's murder, Cain is made a 'vagabond on earth' (*CPW* VI.292). Byron had by this time worked out why Augusta was so lukewarm in her responses to his many previous letters, yet in August 1820 he had told her, 'I always loved you better than any earthly existence, and I always shall unless I go mad' (*BLJ* VII.159).

Southey's use of 'Satanic' seems appropriate in that Lucifer is one of the principal characters of *Cain* and in Act II takes its protagonist on a guided tour of not only present worlds but the remnants of those past. The figure in charge of them all has an omnipotence which Lucifer resents: 'I have a Victor – true, but no superior./ Homage he has from all – but none from me' (*CPW* VI.274). This same defiant spirit is apparent in Cain in the climax of the play when he reluctantly sets up an altar alongside that of Abel for the sacrifice of the offerings he has striven hard to produce. But he ponders why he has to be so thankful for the life of labour to which he is now committed as a result of his expulsion from Eden and given the way a sin for which he himself has not been responsible should have introduced sickness and death as the inevitable end point of that labour. 'What have we/ Done, that we must be victims for a deed/ Before our birth,' he asks, and claims that the sacrifices the brothers are about to make come from fear rather than disinterested worship, that they are 'a bribe/ To the Creator' (*CPW* VI.279). When those sacrifices are in progress, his refusal to kneel initiates a struggle with his brother from which (as the Bible tells us) Abel dies. In part because of his club foot and a temperament that often found him struggling with depression, Byron saw no particular reason for being thankful for the life he had been given, in spite of what, for others, might have seemed its remarkable social advantages.

Goethe complained that whenever Byron reflected, he was like a child and, although he was surprisingly widely read in theological criticism, it is true that he was no metaphysician.[4] Yet there is a bold common sense in some of his questioning about 'original sin', and he has a far more interesting approach to matters biblical or celestial than Robert Southey, whose *Vision of Judgement* is an absurd performance, describing George III's progress to eventual 'beatification' in Heaven in a flurry of clichés and tired metaphors. It was with a Horatian geniality that Byron set out to write a riposte to Southey in his own *Vision of Judgement*, the only poem with that title now remembered, and in which he offered to describe, as it were, what actually happened when the spirit of George III arrived at 'Heaven's Gate'. He referred to this poem, which he composed in the September and October following Shelley's visit and while he was making arrangements to join the Gambas in Pisa, as a 'trifle' (*BLJ* VIII.236), but he must have known it was one of the best he ever wrote.

A typical joke comes at its beginning when Byron is describing how slow business has been in heaven since 1788, the start of what he calls 'the Gallic era' (although also the year of his own birth). A logical consequence of this slow traffic is that the angel charged with recording the misdeeds of mankind during this period has been kept so busy, 'That he had stripp'd off both his wings in quills,/ And yet was in arrear of human ills' (*LB* 942). The source of the comedy here is only marginally dependent on the rhyme and Byron's usual verbal playfulness, and much more on the comic *idea*. It is a derivative of the way he has taken a scenario usually treated with fearful reverence (the Last Judgement) and invited his readers to laugh at its implausibilities. It was not that he wanted flatly to deny that judgement could ever take place; but he objected to the confident manner in which Southey had assumed knowledge of its procedures and, above all, of what its results would be in individual cases. The comedy of his treatment therefore represents both a characteristic refusal to be intimidated and a protest against all those holy willies who felt certain they knew what death would bring to themselves.

Byron's burlesque vision of the attempt by George III to enter heaven is skilfully managed and illustrates a certain continuity with his non-comic writing. Whatever one might think of a poem like *The Corsair*, for example, it would be hard to deny that it illustrates not only Byron's ability to tell a good story ('as a tale-teller,' T. S. Eliot once wrote, 'we must rate Byron very high indeed'[5]), but the keen theatrical sense he left so largely in abeyance for his 'classical' dramas. His ability to orchestrate a dramatic moment is clear enough in episodes from *Don Juan*, like the one in which Donna Julia's husband bursts into her bedroom while the young hero is hiding in her bed, the return of Haidée's father in Canto II or Juan finding himself in a harem disguised as a woman. This aspect of Byron's comic writing – theatrical in that it is so strongly reminiscent of the comic dramatists of the eighteenth century he admired – is apparent in *The Vision of Judgement* when George III arrives on a cloud at Heaven's gate, closely followed by Satan and the archangel Michael. The meeting between these last two is very much a scene from a play with Satan responding as might 'an old Castilian' to Michael's 'graceful oriental bend' (*LB* 951). While they negotiate, Byron works up the character of St Peter, who is grumpy and bored at having so little to do. Largely absent from the debate going on between the two principals, he is roused to comic indignation when Satan, who is arguing against George III's admittance to heaven, points out that the dead king had opposed Catholic emancipation, thereby oppressing the very people most likely to revere Peter's own sainthood: 'Ere Heaven shall ope her portals to this Guelf,/ While I am guard, may I be damn'd myself!', he exclaims (*LB* 954).

Every poet could be described as having a remarkable way with words, but Byron's (unlike Wordsworth's) predisposes him to comic linguistic effect. He adds to that a strong feeling for situations which have comic potential and an understanding of what makes for comedy in human character. Yet crucial to the success of his poem is Byron's maintenance of a general tone which allows him to keep within bounds the occasional savagery of its political satire. That Louis XVI was guillotined does not excuse him, in Byron's view, from having been a bad king, and his arrival at Heaven's gate is an occasion for broad fun: he 'ne'er would have got into heaven's good graces,' complains Peter, 'Had he not flung his head in all our faces' (*LB* 946). There are some heavy blows struck in the description of the funeral of George III, including the often-quoted 'it seem'd the mockery of hell to fold/ The rottenness of eighty years in gold' (*LB* 944); but those are aimed more against the hypocrisy of State functions than George himself, and he ensures that none of them are too damaging to the overall comic mood, that comic spirit which the narrative voice engenders. And it is, after all, a demonstration of the comic spirit in its more conventional sense of general tolerance that, by the end of the poem, George has managed to follow Louis' example and slip into heaven. Byron was furious with Southey for having invited the authorities to persecute writers like himself and declaimed in a preface he wrote for his poem against 'the gross flattery, the dull impudence, and renegado intolerance and impious cant' of Southey's *Vision* (*LB* 939), but his own version is made all the more effective by his ability to keep this kind of anger in control.

9

Pisa and Genoa

The property Shelley had secured for Byron in Pisa was known as the Palazzo Lanfranchi and, had there been the slightest chance Augusta would or could have accepted the invitation he now sent her to join him there (*BLJ* IX.57), was big enough to have accommodated his sister along with her children and the man Byron called her 'drone of a husband'. The Gambas' residence was nearby and so was the Shelleys', so the same kind of close communication Byron had enjoyed with Shelley in Geneva might therefore have been re-established were the circumstances not now so different. For one thing, a group of other English-speakers with literary interests had also been attracted to Pisa, in the first instance and in part because of Shelley's presence there. These included, or eventually would include, Shelley's cousin Thomas Medwin, an ex-army officer called Edward Williams and Edward Trelawny, who had been in the Royal Navy. These three may have admired Shelley's writing but they admired that of the far more celebrated Byron as least as much if not more: Trelawny claimed to have slept with *The Corsair* under his pillow, and based his flamboyant public persona on the hero of that poem. With his large premises and substantial income, it was Byron who became the chief focus of the group; Shelley must have quickly discovered he could not have his friend to himself, as had more or less been the case in Switzerland.

Byron had been starved of the company of young English-speaking men and rapidly organized a series of all-male weekly dinners at Lanfranchi in which a good deal of drinking went on. Since the Pisan authorities refused his request to practise pistol shooting in his own garden, he also organized regular excursions out of town to a farm where he and his new friends could fire away with impunity. This was his afternoon exercise, which in Ravenna had usually involved horse-riding alone and in Venice lots of swimming. Those of the Pisan group who were still alive when Byron died profited from his celebrity by writing reminiscences of him. They reported what a jovial and engaging host he could be, constantly witty and full of anecdotes about the writers and politicians he had known in London. But some observed also that he did not much enjoy extended intellectual discussion. This was unlike Shelley, who was much more adept at it, but no great drinker, so the weekly dinners were not a particularly happy experience for him. But there were multiple other reasons for Shelley's growing alienation, one of which, he freely admitted, was his frustration at Byron's continuing success in the publishing world at a time when knowledge of his own work remained confined to a small circle.

Yet Shelley never stopped believing that the man he had been instrumental in bringing to Pisa was a great poet, and it was an especial comfort to Byron that he admired not only *Don Juan* but *Cain*. This was because they were two works that his friends and foes back in London were unanimous in thinking should never have been published. When an attack on both appeared in the *Edinburgh Review* in February 1822, Byron was upset because he knew the author was Jeffrey, whom he had come to both like and admire. This article took *Don Juan* as an example of the tendency in Byron's writing to 'destroy all belief in the reality of virtue'. It also described his classical dramas (with rather more justice) as 'heavy, verbose and inelegant', full of 'pompous declamation', while complaining that in *Cain* he was treating issues that were really the province of theologians and philosophers. 'Poetical dreamers and

Palazzo Toscanelli (formerly Lanfranchi) in Pisa, from Peter Brent, *Lord Byron* (1974).

sophists who pretend to *theorise* according to their feverish fancies, without a warrant from authority or reason,' Jeffrey insisted, 'ought to be banished the commonwealth of letters.'[1]

Teresa may have put a temporary hold on more *Don Juan*, but adverse public criticism was never likely to stop Byron in his tracks. Following on from *Cain*, he wrote another of what he now termed 'mysteries', after the medieval dramas with religious themes which went by that name. This was called *Heaven and Earth* and dealt with the situation on Earth just before the Deluge (an alternative title). Two sisters, who are descendants of Cain, have fallen in love with angels, while one of Noah's sons, Japhet, still retains a hopeless longing for one of them. The action focuses in part on how self-sacrificial love can be, although there is in the piece enough unorthodox treatment of religious themes to make Murray nervous about publication, particularly after the loud protests *Cain* had prompted, and it had to wait eighteen months before it appeared in the second number of the radical journal Byron and Shelley had been planning.

Heaven and Earth was no more meant for the theatre than Byron's 'classical' dramas, but he followed it up with a play that could easily have been staged, and which at least showed his versatility. This was based on a story that had impressed him when he was a boy and concerns a bitter and impoverished aristocrat, known only at first as Werner, who is struggling with his wife to keep body and soul together in an old, decayed German castle, shortly after the Thirty Years War (1618–48). The death of his father means that his troubles are about to be over, but, when the very relative who is trying to bar Werner from his inheritance happens to be staying with him in the castle and is murdered, the play becomes a whodunit, no worse than (and not very different from) the many plays Byron must have seen or read at Drury Lane. What Byron's expectations for this work were are not entirely clear but, along with pistol shooting and hosting dinners, not to mention the hours he spent every day with Teresa,

Charles Williams, 'A Noble Poet, Scratching up his Ideas', 1823, satirical print.

writing it kept him occupied and reasonably contented. When Trelawny mentioned a scheme they had all previously conceived to have a boat built and sail together on the Ligurian Sea once the summer arrived, Byron was keen to join in and arranged to have a boat built for himself as well, indicating that he did not mind it being costly since he was now beginning to feel well-off. This was because his mother-in-law had died and, according to the marriage and separation settlements, the considerable income from her estates was to be divided between him and Lady Byron. He believed this would mean an extra £3,000 or £4,000 a year but the details took a long time to be worked out, so that when he discovered that the building of the boat (which he called the *Bolivar*) was going to cost him not the £300 he had anticipated but more than three times that amount, he was not pleased. An offshoot of the death of his mother-in-law, Lady Noel, was that he was now obliged to sign himself Noel Byron or NB, which, as he liked to remind people, were the same initials as Napoleon's.

The pleasant routines into which Byron had settled in Pisa were soon disrupted by a series of misfortunes. The first came in March when the shooting party was riding back into town, preceded by a carriage Teresa and Mary Shelley had used to keep an eye on their menfolk. A soldier who was in a hurry, and who may have found that these foreigners were taking up too much of the road, rudely bustled past them on his horse. Byron was one of those who galloped after him and there was an altercation at the city's gate that quickly developed into a scuffle as the soldier attempted to have them all arrested. There resulted only minor injuries to two of the English party (including Shelley) while the soldier was far more seriously wounded by one of Byron's servants. It was a case of road rage with major consequences, since the Tuscan authorities, already worried about the presence of the Gambas and Byron in Pisa, became even more anxious to get rid of both. Why this mattered became more obvious when Byron adopted the same Italian habit of *villeggiatura* he had practised in Venice, moving out of town in the summer to avoid the heat. He rented a large house with a view on the sea near Leghorn, but after he and the Gambas moved there, in May 1822, the residence permits of the latter were revoked and a search began for where else they could next go. Meanwhile, although Byron's boat was now complete, the authorities imposed such severe restrictions on where along the coastline it could sail that, with its four small cannons mounted on the deck, it became unusable. This cast a damper on his participation in the summer sailing schemes, which Shelley and Williams had already begun to implement by moving their families to a large house further up the coast from Leghorn at Lerici.

It was only about three weeks before Byron's move to Leghorn when the second misfortune occurred and he received the news that

Allegra had died. She had clearly not been ill-treated and the nuns had been kind (spoiled her, in fact). When her fever had declared itself, Byron ordered the best medical treatment, yet he nevertheless must have felt some guilt, especially about not having paid this five-year-old girl a visit before he left the Ravenna area. He left to Shelley the difficult task of breaking the bad news to Allegra's mother. Claire had, in fact, been intermittently in Pisa without his knowledge, continually complaining about her inability to see her daughter and protesting against her being cooped up with nuns. Although Shelley had endorsed Byron's decision to send her to the convent school, he may now have begun to switch to Claire's side as his hostility to Byron grew and he became more aware of their ideological differences. He increasingly felt that Byron was full of aristocratic prejudices and became exasperated at how woolly he could be when it came to metaphysical issues. 'I do believe, Mary,' Trelawny reports him as saying at one point, 'that he is little better than a Christian.'[2]

Yet Shelley appears to have conveyed little sense of these hostile feelings to Byron himself, and the scheme for a liberal journal was still alive. So much alive that Byron had already provided the £250 required to bring Leigh Hunt and his family over to Italy so that, with his experience of editing *The Examiner* and his publishing contacts in London, as well as his own writing skills, he could help with the launch (it was having to arrange this 'loan' from Byron that seems to have increased Shelley's dislike of him). After many delays, Hunt arrived in Leghorn at a bad moment for Byron, with the Gambas just about to receive an order to quit the territory. They hoped to find sanctuary in Lucca, but meanwhile Byron headed back to Pisa so that he could install Hunt, his wife and their six children in the bottom storey of the Palazzo Lanfranchi while Teresa stayed on by herself in the house with him, thereby abandoning all pretence about the real nature of their relationship. It was in Pisa that news came of another major misfortune: Shelley,

Williams and a young boy they had taken with them as crew had been caught in a storm while sailing back from Leghorn to Lerici and all had drowned. This was devastating information on so many fronts, a minor one of which was that there was now no buffer between Byron and Hunt, who were not destined to get on. Yet the animosity seems to have been much more on Hunt's side, as it had been on Shelley's in his relationship with Byron. Writing to Murray about the drowning, Byron insisted: 'You are all brutally mistaken about Shelley who was without exception – the *best* and least selfish man I ever knew – I never knew one who was not a beast in comparison –' (*BLJ* IX.189–90).

The succeeding weeks were spent in rapidly deteriorating relations with the Hunt family (Byron kept their six unruly children at bay by posting his bulldog at the top of the stairs that led to his own apartments), although with Hunt himself, whom he had known and liked when he was in London, he seems to have been stimulated by political discussions which strengthened his essentially republican sympathies. There were also macabre expeditions with Trelawny and others to cremate the bodies of Williams and Shelley – which had washed up on the Ligurian shore – in Shelley's case so that his ashes could be collected and deposited in the Roman cemetery where one of his sons had been buried. Meanwhile the search for a place where the Gambas would be accepted continued, since the authorities in Lucca were about to decide against allowing them to stay. Pre-unified Italy was at this period a patchwork of different administrations, and it was eventually in Genoa, then in the control of the kingdom of Sardinia, that a house was found for them all.

The deaths of Allegra and Shelley had hardly improved Byron's spirits, and more than ever he needed the distraction of writing. He had in fact begun to work again on *Don Juan* before Teresa had eventually relented and given him official permission (as it were) to carry on. She might have regretted this had she realized that his treatment of 'romantic' love was no less ironic than it had been before and that, as he described how his disguised hero fared in the harem, his sense of the way in which love relates to sex was even less idealistic in this sixth canto than it had been in the previous five. After some daring lines about how much play-acting might have to be involved now that the sultan had unexpectedly arrived to sleep with his favourite wife, among so many others on offer – how much Gulbayez, that is, might have to fake it – there is lively sex comedy as three of the other women in the harem eagerly put themselves forward to share their bed with 'Juanna' (given that, as a newcomer to the scene, she is presumed to be nervous). The girl chosen is called Dodù and everyone is woken up when she is heard crying out loudly in the middle of the night. They then gather round to ask what the matter is, but she claims to have been awoken by a dream and fiercely resists any suggestion that Juanna, who is meanwhile apparently still sound asleep, should be moved to someone else's bed. When Gulbayez learns of these incidents in the morning, she immediately understands what has happened and, in a jealous fury, makes arrangements for having Dodù and Juan sown into sacks and thrown into the sea. All this is very effectively related in a comic manner, full of striking descriptions; but it has a freedom which suggests that Byron was no longer going to worry about those critics in England who considered him licentious, and he did not much care whether Murray would be prepared to publish this continuation of *Don Juan*. After all, through Leigh Hunt he now had another contact, Hunt's brother John, who was still editing *The Examiner* at home and who would take on the task of publishing in October the first number of the radical journal Byron and Shelley had always been planning. It was called *The Liberal* and it was to this first number that Byron contributed *The Vision of Judgement*, without any immediate expectation of payment.

   This gradual cutting of ties with the more conventional publishing world Murray represented coincides with Byron deciding to be much freer in both the expression of his political views and his dealing with sexual issues. In the two cantos after the scenes in the harem (where a war between the Turks and Russians has already been mentioned), he assumes that Juan has somehow escaped the fate Gulbayez was preparing for him and made his way to the city of Ismail on the Danube, which, in 1790, was besieged by a Russian army led by General Suvaroff. This is so he can express, much more strongly than he had before, his horror at what man can do to man in warfare. Byron's attitude to what he calls repeatedly 'glory' had always been ambivalent. On the one hand, he was keen to distinguish himself in ways other than literary, but, on the other, he felt that most wars were the pastime of autocratic rulers who did not really care about the horrendous consequences, brought to either their own populations or those of others, of their selfish pursuit of conquest. The exceptions he mentions were generals like George Washington, who was involved in a war of liberation, or King Leonidas, the leader of the three hundred Spartans who held the Persians at bay at Thermopylae. His admiration for the Americans had been bolstered by a warm and flattering welcome he had received when he was invited to visit some of their ships anchored in Leghorn's harbour; and since the Greek war of independence had broken out in 1821, his mind often reverted to the idea of going back to Greece and doing what he could to help.

Byron took his knowledge of the Ismail siege from a French account, skilfully incorporating into his verse all the technical details of siege warfare and sparing his reader none of the gory details of the wholesale slaughter which the capture of the town involved. But the mode in which his descriptions are cast remains essentially comic. He said that what he was doing was no different from the tone he had adopted when describing the shipwreck and its aftermath in Canto II. This description, he suggested, had been much admired, although in the *Edinburgh Review* article that upset Byron, Jeffrey had written that 'the sublime and terrific description of the Shipwreck is strangely and disgustingly broken by traits of low humour and buffoonery.'[3] But there are essential differences between the two cases. The shipwreck is a clear example of dark humour, with all the theoretical difficulty that raises, whereas, in these new warfare cantos, there is a clear satirical intention which determines the tone as Byron seeks to illustrate the realities of a violence for which he holds autocratic rulers such as, in this instance, Catherine the Great, responsible. The humour is a sardonic response to a distribution of political and, by extension, military power of which Byron vehemently disapproves, even if it also relates to an underlying despair about not only the behaviour of human beings in general, but the purpose of their lives.

This last feeling stems from what, well before Schopenhauer, could be called Byron's nihilism, an approach or attitude for which he was frequently criticized. At the beginning of Canto VII, he is no longer deterred from expressing this openly: 'Must I refrain me, through the fear of strife/ From holding up the Nothingness of Life?' (*LB* 622). But the idea that human behaviour is a wretched affair in general does not prevent him from identifying a number of individuals whom he feels need to be criticized for encouraging or facilitating its excesses. Towards the end of his account, he reverts to the British political scene as he is contrasting the ambition to have one's name recorded in the gazette (to be mentioned in dispatches) with the brutal reality the siege of Ismail illustrates. 'Think how the joys of reading a Gazette', stanza 125 of Canto VIII begins, 'Are purchased by all agonies and crimes'. British readers are not, moreover, he goes on in this stanza, as far removed from future situations at home which may eventually lead to those same agonies and crimes as they may think, especially if they pay attention to the current desperate situation in Ireland: 'Read your own hearts and Ireland's present story/ Then feed her famine fat with Wellesley's glory' (*LB* 673). Wellesley, or the Duke of Wellington as he became known, was Irish, and Byron thought it scandalous that this widely celebrated hero should be so apparently indifferent to the troubles of his homeland. Even stronger was his criticism of another Irishman prominent in Westminster politics – but then Castlereagh was someone Byron hated so much that, in a ferocious preface he wrote for these new cantos of *Don Juan*, he could dismiss the idea that he should be spoken about any less severely because he happened to have committed suicide recently. After all, what Castlereagh had illustrated in cutting his throat with a penknife was that sometimes men 'judge so justly of their own actions as to anticipate the sentence of mankind' (*LB* 590). His record on Irish affairs had also been deplorable, although the Irish themselves, he ironically tells them in a stanza following the reference to Wellington, should not worry too much as 'Desolation/ Strips your green fields and to your harvests cling'. This is because 'Gaunt famine never shall approach the throne –/ Though Ireland starve, great George weighs twenty stone' (*LB* 674). There is a degree of sarcasm here, directed at the notoriously fat George IV, which Murray would have been very reluctant to publish. After all, Byron had first met Leigh Hunt after he and his brother had been sent to prison for being rude in print about George when he was Prince Regent.

The house Byron rented in Genoa was in a suburb called Albaro, but it had views of the sea and was large enough for both him and the Gambas to have their separate establishments. Leigh Hunt also moved to Genoa, along with his family, and so did Mary Shelley, who, with the death of her husband, was suddenly cast adrift. As an executor of Shelley's will, Byron wrote an excellent letter to Mary's father-in-law asking him to consider providing an allowance for her and her young son (*BLJ* X.78–9), and he continued to help Hunt in small ways while complaining that doing so was like pulling a man out of the river only to see him throw himself back in again. The ostensible reason of their being together was so that they might collaborate on the new journal, part of whose purpose, in

Shelley's mind, had always been that it would provide Hunt with a steady income. The first number of *The Liberal* came out in October 1822, with Byron's *Vision of Judgement* as its leading item and a fiery preface by Hunt. Predictably enough, this first number was badly received, one reviewer claiming that Byron's contribution had been 'impiety, vulgarity, inhumanity and heartlessness' while Hunt had then added 'conceit, trumpery, ignorance and wretched verses'.[4] But the chief target was *The Vision of Judgement*, the publication of which led to Leigh Hunt's brother John being prosecuted. The action was brought not directly by the government but by an organization called the Constitutional Association. As soon as he heard about it, Byron instructed Kinnaird to engage an expensive lawyer and several times offered to travel to England in order to face the music himself. But Hunt felt that would do no good, nor affect the final result, which came in 1824 and was a fine of £100, paid by Kinnaird from the Byron estate.

All Byron's friends in England strongly disapproved of *The Liberal* and his association with the Hunts, but poor though his relations with Leigh were, he did not feel he could leave him in the lurch. Money was at the root of the problem. Leigh Hunt appears to have believed that a man as rich as Byron ought to be more carelessly open-handed, while Mary Shelley probably had similar feelings, especially when she was trying to persuade him that he should provide some kind of annual allowance for her half-sister, Claire. But Byron had long ago determined to have nothing whatever to do with Allegra's mother, and both Mary and Hunt were unlucky in knowing him at a period when he was taking an increasingly close interest in the sources of his income. He had cut down his own expenses, selling half his horses and reducing the number of his servants, and taken control of his own household accounts. When Kinnaird suggested that some of the money he had begun to accumulate could be used to finally pay off his remaining debts, which still amounted to about £2,000, he dug in his heels and argued against giving up such a large lump sum. His aim seems to have been to collect together a nest egg of £10,000 which he could then rely on should the government stocks from which much of his income came collapsed (an eventuality he was always predicting). But it was also that he felt he needed a lot of ready cash available should he decide to emigrate to South America and buy an estate there; or if he wanted to go to Greece and do what he could to help since, as he says in one of his letters from this period, monies are 'the 'Sinews of War' (*BLJ* X.114).

Byron remained close enough to Mary Shelley to ask her to produce fair copies of what he was writing, as she already had done in Switzerland. Even more than the new cantos of *Don Juan* he was now composing, Mary admired a play he began at this time but never finished called *The Deformed Transformed*, which concerns a hunchback named Arnold who makes a pact with the Devil that allows him to exchange his own disabled body for a more brilliantly healthy one. What is most biographically interesting in this uncompleted text is its opening scene, in which Arnold's mother cries 'Out! Hunchback' while her son responds mildly with 'I was born so, Mother!' 'Out / Thou incubus! Thou nightmare! Of seven sons,/ The sole abortion!', she then replies (*CPW* VI.519). A little later on there are lines that indicate Byron had forgotten that the disability he had given Arnold involves his back and not his foot. That Byron remained acutely conscious of his club foot all his life is obvious enough. Teresa Guiccioli recalled how he spoke to her about the anguish it had always caused him, but another woman to whom he unburdened himself on the subject was Lady Blessington, which is surprising given that she was a new acquaintance. She was passing through Genoa with her husband on a leisurely, extended continental tour and Byron was taken with her charm and sympathetic intelligence. If it is to Moore that we owe Byron's report that his mother once called him a lame brat, it is Lady Blessington who describes how when he was a child insults of this kind made him 'rush into solitude, where, unseen, I could vent the rage and mortification I endured, and curse the deformity that I now began to consider as a signal mark of the injustice of Providence'.[5]

The Blessingtons were such a valuable social resource for Byron that he tried to persuade them to settle in Genoa longer than they intended. With them, he could not only speak English but remind himself of the upper-class social scene of which he had once been a part and which had now become the subject of *Don Juan*. After the siege of Ismail, his young hero is taken to Moscow and becomes the official lover of Catherine the Great. Partly due to the rigours of that role, he falls ill and is then dispatched to Britain on a diplomatic mission. British social life thus becomes the main subject of the new cantos. Yet if this chimes in with the arrival of the Blessingtons, an encounter of more obvious general significance came when in April 1823 he was able to meet, in this case only briefly, a former naval officer called Edward Blaquiere. He was accompanied by a member of the Greek provisional government and was part of an effort to establish in London a 'Greek committee' to co-ordinate British efforts to further Greece's independence. Blaquiere wanted not only to make Byron a member of this committee, but to explore with him the idea of his going to Greece in order to establish what kind of help the Greeks needed and where whatever money the committee could raise would be best spent. As Byron himself recognized, the time he had spent in Greece, his sympathy for any nation struggling to gain its independence, and his command of Italian, made him the kind of high-profile figure eminently suited for this role.

From the time of Blaquiere's visit onwards, Byron began making preparations for this journey, one of which involved selling the *Bolivar* to Lord Blessington for about half its construction cost (the more money he had available, the better). He bought a fair number of medical supplies, engaged a private doctor to accompany him and persuaded Trelawny to come to Greece also. But his major problem was, of course, Teresa. Rejecting firmly her urgent request that she accompany him into what was effectively a war zone, Byron was helped enormously by the fact that Teresa's brother Pietro, a fiery young man who had been disappointed that he had not yet had the opportunity to fight for Italian unification, and who was warmly attached to Byron, was even keener to go to Greece than he was. That Teresa could anticipate hearing about Byron from her brother must have been a comfort to her. At this period also, Count Gamba's exile had been revoked and he was free to return to Ravenna and take his daughter with him. But she at first insisted she would stay in Genoa to await her lover's return, either in a convent or under the protection of some pious old lady. Although Byron made some efforts to make the necessary arrangements, they proved too difficult to work out and she eventually had to accept the inevitable. It was often said later that Byron was anxious to make the trip to Greece because it extricated him from an awkward situation. There may be a modicum of truth in this, and his previous passionate love for Teresa had certainly moderated into a quasi-marital fondness. But the presence of Pietro at his side in Greece suggests he had no intention of deserting her and that he always intended to return when it seemed appropriate to do so.

The Greek venture may have provided Byron with an opportunity to extricate himself from his relationship with Teresa, but far more certain is that it allowed him to cease his support for *The Liberal* and end his uneasy contacts with the Hunts, who otherwise were in danger of becoming his semi-permanent financial dependants. To the second number, which appeared at the end of 1822, he contributed his *Heaven and Earth*, and in the third, published at the beginning of the next year, there was *The Blues*, two opening scenes only of a would-be comic playlet which featured various members of the more intellectual circles Byron had moved in when he was last in England, the main interest of which nowadays lies in readers trying to work out who is meant to be whom. By the time of this third number, it was clear that *The Liberal* was not going to make money, and in the fourth and last Byron's translation of Pulci appeared, along with the original Italian. But by that time, he was on his way to Greece.

One positive result for Byron of *The Liberal* was the strengthening of his bond with John Hunt, with whom he seems to have got along much more harmoniously (if only by letter) than with his brother Leigh. Two works which Byron might first have considered for this journal but decided would fare better as separate publications were *The Age of Bronze* and *The Island*. Now that he had split from Murray it was useful that Hunt was willing to take charge of both. *The Age of Bronze* was a satirical account in heroic couplets of the state of Europe after the defeat and then death of Napoleon. Most likely prompted by a congress held in Verona by the major autocratic powers of Europe in November 1822, this poem reviewed the reactionary state Europe had fallen into after Napoleon's defeat and gave an account of the efforts of countries like Spain to establish a more democratic government, and of those like Greece who were struggling to establish their independence. With some shrewd hits, but little humour, it is a somewhat leaden affair. *The Island* is a quite different work. At the beginning of *The Age of Bronze*, Byron writes 'Reader! remember when thou wert a lad', although his early success had been based on a wide female readership. It was about this time that he contemptuously reported to friends how Murray had asked whether he could not write 'a poem in the old way to interest the women' (*BLJ* IX.125). There were political, sexual and (above all, perhaps) religious reasons why his work was no longer so popular with women and why his sale figures had dropped so considerably from what they had been at the time of *Childe Harold* and the Turkish tales, but *The Island* is certainly not written with what are regarded as exclusively male interests in mind.

This could seem surprising given that the subject of the poem is the mutiny on the *Bounty*. One might have expected Byron to side with the mutineers, given his own strong inclination to support any rebellion against authority, but his attitude is ambivalent, perhaps on account of his own naval background but more obviously because his major source for the details of the event is the one which Bligh, the *Bounty*'s captain, had recently published. Byron's chief focus is on what happened to the mutineers once they had settled on their island in the Pacific, and in particular on the fate of a young Scot whom he names Torquil and who forms a relationship with a local girl called Neuha. This allows Byron to write evocative as well as highly romanticized lines about love in a state of nature, somewhat like those in the second canto of *Don Juan* about the love between his young hero and Haidée. But the relationship between Torquil and Neuha is interrupted when a British warship appears. It is then that Neuha ushers Torquil into a canoe and, pursued by the new arrivals, heads towards a nearby island, which appears to consist of nothing more than high, impassable rocks. She then dives into the sea and, encouraging her lover to do the same, shows him how it is possible to swim through a narrow underwater opening in the rock and access what, in the middle of this apparently inhospitable island, is an inner sanctum of safety. When they eventually reappear, it is to find that Torquil is the last surviving mutineer but is now free to resume his love affair with Neuha. There is, of course, no reason why female readers should be considered more sentimental that their male counterparts but at least they are not excluded from reading *The Island* by having to remember back to a time when they were lads.

The quantity and variety of Byron's writing during this final phase in Italy is extraordinary, especially given that he was also racing along with *Don Juan*. From the point of Juan's arrival in London in the middle of Canto X, Byron wrote six more cantos and the beginning of what would have been a seventeenth. During the course of them, his narrative method changes in a way analogous to what had happened in *Childe Harold*. That is to say that the narrative voice becomes much more obviously his own, without the cover of an invented or implied persona, and in many places even more overtly autobiographical than before. This is partly because of a change in subject-matter. The previous cantos were full of episodes of which, in the main, he had no direct personal experience (shipwrecks, sieges and so on), but now, in bringing his hero to London on a diplomatic mission and introducing him to upper-class English society, he was dealing with his own quite recent past. His poem therefore becomes part of a re-evaluation of what it had meant for a young man to suddenly find himself on the invitation lists of nearly all the fashionable hostesses of the day – 'the major difference' being that Juan's popularity has nothing to do with being a writer.

Juan has come to London with a young Muslim girl whom he saved from the siege at Ismail and who features in the poem as a surrogate daughter or younger sister; but her care is soon transferred to an old lady in order that he can be described as participating untrammelled in the social life of the capital. There are brilliant accounts of what that involved as well as of prominent physical features of London, but also numerous long and fascinating digressions as Byron ponders his past. Noting that the only attraction Juan lacks for the fashionable social world is that he is not a poet, for example, leads Byron to recall 'a considerable time' when he himself was reckoned 'The grand Napoleon of the realms of rhyme' (*LB* 734). This brings him to a review of the current literary scene, which lasts for seven stanzas, before Juan's story is picked up again. Contemplating how social life can lead rich young aristocrats to fritter away their time until 'having voted, dined, drunk, gamed and whored,/ The family vault receives another Lord' (*LB* 739), Byron is led into a second, longer digression about the changes that have taken place since he was last in London, some of these relating to particular individuals but others to groups, like the women he used to know:

> Some who once set their caps at cautious dukes,
>   Have taken up at length with younger brothers:
> Some heiresses have bit at sharper's hooks:
>   Some maids have been made wives, some merely
>   mothers: . . . (*LB* 738)

Always acutely aware of passing time, it shocked Byron to realize from the letters and reports he received, and from travellers like Lady Blessington, how much of the London world he had recently known was no longer there.

Canto XII begins with a long reflection on the importance of money – worthy of comparison with the opening of Ben Jonson's *Volpone* – and is followed by a lively critique of the annual marriage market in upper-class circles. As a handsome foreigner presumed to be wealthy, Juan attracts the attention of several women but particularly two who happen to be already married. One of these is the promiscuous Duchess of Fitz-Fulke and the other the more respectable Lady Adeline, who disguises her own attraction to Juan by telling herself that she needs to protect the naive young man from sexual predators like Fitz-Fulke. There is a subtlety of psychological analysis in her delineation reminiscent of Jane Austen and the way the latter part of *Don Juan* develops is in fact much like a novel. Austen seems an appropriate name to mention because, after the London 'season' is over, Lady Adeline and her husband invite Juan down to their country seat, which Byron describes in some detail (relying on his memories of Newstead Abbey). It is in this former monastery, with many of its surviving medieval appurtenances, that the action takes place, including an encounter with a ghost, so that the novels to which *Don Juan* starts to approximate here are those of the 'Gothic' variety which Austen began her career by parodying in *Northanger Abbey*. Yet the more apt comparison is not so much with Austen but with predecessors such as Fanny Burney or Maria Edgeworth, since the influence on them of eighteenth-century picaresque novelists like Fielding or Smollet is much more obvious. As far as *Don Juan*'s specifically English literary heritage is concerned, one of its achievements is to have been able to combine the rumbustious good humour of writers like Fielding with the sharp and sometimes acid wit of Pope.

Byron's psychological acuteness is not limited to his female portraits, none of which are very obvious versions of the women he had known, but extends also to male figures such as Lady Adeline's husband. He is not unsympathetically presented as more interested in politics than his wife and engrossed with the tasks of running a large estate. There are excellent descriptions of what this involves as well as of a huge banquet he feels he must give in order to ensure that all those in the surrounding area who are entitled to vote are kept happy. Also impressive are vivid accounts of hunting parties and the other diversions employed to alleviate the crushing boredom that can afflict the members of a country house party as an English winter begins to set in. However, that Juan is intrigued not so much by Lady Adeline or Fitz-Fulke but by an aloof young woman called Aurora keeps the love interest predominant and, despite the many digressions, the plot is developing nicely when, with Byron's imminent departure for Greece, the poem suddenly and disappointedly breaks off. That he was never able or minded to return to it, and *Don Juan* remained unfinished, does not make it any less a great work. There are inevitably in its thousands of lines one or two slack or dull passages, but on the whole the quality is remarkably consistent. Discussing the *ottava rima* verse form, a leading Byron authority has suggested that 'the stanza almost always sounds contrived.'[6] It is true that Byron sometimes draws attention to the form he is using by the comic ingenuity of his rhyming, yet in general it seems to me that the impression he miraculously conveys is of relaxed ease and naturalness, as if one were listening to his conversation, which, as the reports testify, was animated, insightful and above all funny.

It is the comedy consistently present in *Don Juan* that makes the work difficult to talk about. The aspect easiest to illustrate is the epigrammatic neatness often found in the final couplets of the stanzas, but it takes many other different forms. His wife thought he was flippant and, in her memoir of him, Lady Blessington also concluded: 'Were I asked to point out the prominent defect of Byron, I should say it was flippancy.'[7] But this is a word we tend to associate with shallow natures, whereas it is impossible to read *Don Juan* for long without noticing that much of its comedy arises from a realization of how far the world we live in falls short of our hopes and expectations, and that the only reasonable response means finding many aspects of it ridiculous or absurd.

10

Epilogue

In a vessel he had rented for his expedition to Greece, Byron left Genoa in July 1823. With him was a small group of servants as well as Francesco Bruno, the private doctor he had recently engaged. Pietro Gamba and Trelawny were, of course, on board but the ship was also carrying a number of animals, including Bryon's favourite dog, as well as the various medical and military supplies the group thought would be useful to bring along. On 3 August, the expedition reached Cephalonia, one of the Ionian Islands under British control. Although Trelawny quickly moved on from there, Byron decided to settle in for a while so that he could assess the political and military situation from a safe distance.

One entirely valid reason for doing this was a conflict among the Greek leaders so serious that it would occasionally lead to their fighting each other rather than the Turks. He became anxious that they should resolve their disagreements, aware of how damaging these could be for the efforts to raise a large loan certain officials of the provisional government were about to make in London. In the meantime, he lent the Greeks around £3,000 of his own money, which they said they needed, principally in order to pay the sailors of their fleet: it was the inactivity of their ships that had allowed the Turks to maintain a blockade between the Ionian Islands and the Greek mainland.

To a loan he had to assume he might never get back, he quickly began to add a number of other expenses, although with a heart made lighter than it might have been after he heard that his Rochdale estate had finally been sold and more than £11,000 would soon be in his bank account. The Ionian Islands were full of refugees of one kind or another and Byron made a point of providing money for both sides, Muslims and Christians. In one Greek family he helped there was a handsome fifteen-year-old boy called Loukas whom he took on as his page, as he had Nicolo Giraud a decade previously. Present in larger numbers were also Souliotes, members of a Christian sect from Albania whom Byron had come across and admired as fierce warriors when he visited Ali Pasha in 1809. Having been finally prised out of their mountain stronghold, the surviving Souliotes had dispersed themselves over the adjacent areas and Byron began putting some of them on his payroll in order to form a bodyguard or small private army. The news of his presence in Cephalonia, and of the apparently unlimited financial resources he seemed to have at his disposal, spread quickly and probably helped to motivate the approaches he began to receive from various contending Greek leaders. The one to which he eventually decided to respond came from Alexander Mavrocordatos, the ousted former President of the National Assembly of the provisional Greek government who was now on his way to Missolonghi as the governor of western Greece. The attraction of the invitation to join him no doubt lay partly in the fact that Missolonghi was on the edge of the Greek mainland, not many hours sailing from Cephalonia; but principally in Byron having heard good things about Mavrocordatos from the Shelleys, who had known him when he was an exile in Pisa and had given Mary lessons in Greek. At the end of December 1823, Byron and Pietro set out for Missolonghi in different boats and were lucky to arrive there relatively unscathed. Pietro's vessel, which was carrying money as well as military stores, was temporarily impounded by the Turks, while Byron's own smaller and lighter craft was chased up the coast from the approaches to Missolonghi so that its occupants were forced to finish their journey overland.

Byron's house at Missolonghi, 1830, aquatint.

There were many more Souliotes in Missolonghi than
Cepholonia and Byron began enrolling them until he had five or six
hundred for whom he assumed financial responsibility. Together
with the local Greeks, they became part of a strategy to send an
army to capture the town of Lepanto on the Gulf of Corinth (as
Corinth itself had recently been taken from the Turks, this would
presumably have left the whole gulf free of their control). Perhaps
because Byron was about the only person the unruly Souliotes
would listen to, it was decided that he should be the leader of
this expedition, even though he had no military experience. A
surprising feature of his life at this period is that, since leaving
Genoa, he had more or less stopped writing, but now he composed
a short 'Song to the Suliotes', which begins:

Up to battle! Sons of Suli
Up and do your duty duly!
There the wall – and there the Moat is:
Bouwah! Bouwah! Suliotes!
There is booty – there is Beauty,
Up my boys and do your duty.

Although 'Bouwah' was Byron's version of the Souliotes' war cry, it is doubtful whether many of them had enough English to pay heed to this injunction. Booty and beauty were no doubt major incentives to them but it is strange that Byron should refer to both when, in *Don Juan*, he had been so critical of the pillage and rape that had been associated with the siege of Ismael (one of his rationalizations for accepting the leadership of the proposed Lepanto expedition was that, should its defenders capitulate, he would be there to prevent the kind of atrocities that had already disfigured some recent Greek successes). It was perhaps fortunate that the idea of the attack on Lepanto was dropped. This might have been because, although the Souliotes were formidable guerrilla fighters in their native mountains, siege warfare – the walls and moats Byron refers to – was not their forte. More probable is the fact that they had angered him so much by demanding more money that at one point he dismissed them all before then agreeing to re-engage them on the old terms. And then there was that they had frequently caused trouble in Missolonghi, integrating badly with the local population, and were a likely disruptive presence in any army.

Whatever the reasons, the abandonment of the Lepanto project must have left Byron deeply disillusioned, aware that the heroic warriors he had idealized were in fact self-seeking, and wondering why he had come to Greece if it was only to be exploited. But it was not only public matters that unsettled him at this time. The only other poems he wrote, apart from his 'Song to the Suliotes', were three short lyrics. The first of these was composed on his 36th birthday, in January 1824, and is a reproach to himself to forget about a love he harbours, especially as he knows that it is unreciprocated. 'Tread these reviving passions down,' he writes, and think rather of the Greek cause (*LB* 970). In the other two poems he expresses his unhappiness at still being 'a fool of passion' (*CPW* VII.83) and having fallen in love with someone who has no interest in him. That this is his page Loukas seems reasonably clear.

In one of the poems he refers to an earthquake which in February caused a great deal of alarm and damage in Missolonghi and complains about how little it seems to matter to Loukas that his first thought amid tottering walls had been for him. Yet 'nor can I blame thee', this poem ends, 'though it be my lot/ To strongly – wrongly – vainly – love thee still' (*CPW* VII.82).

Earthquakes were only one of the misfortunes to have hampered Greek efforts in Missolonghi at this time. Another was that it rained very heavily, turning the land in and around the already marshy town into a quagmire. This must have hindered military preparations but also often meant that Byron could not take the exercise he needed to improve his faltering health. In the months leading up to his death in April, there had been two disturbing episodes, during both of which he lost control of his body, collapsed on the floor and was incoherent for several hours. The doctors with him at the time diagnosed these as epileptic seizures, although he had no previous history of epilepsy and they may well have been physical responses to the enormous pressures he was then under, having daily to deal with requests for more financial help from so many different quarters, as well as his Souliotes. Easier to identify – although accurate medical diagnosis is impossible at this distance in time – is the fever he began to suffer from in April. The last time he was in western Greece, and shortly before he left for England, he had been very ill with what was almost certainly malaria and tenderly nursed through his sickness by Nicolo Giraud (a role that his new page Loukas was obviously not minded or fitted to play). In Venice also, where malaria was endemic, he had been dangerously ill with a fever on at least one occasion and boasted afterwards that what had saved him had been the absence of doctors. The fever which struck him down in April in Missolonghi is likely to have been malarial also, but this time there was not only Dr Bruno in close attendance but a Dr Millingen, who had been sent out to help by the London Greek Committee. Both these medical specialists were believers in the then orthodox treatment of bleeding for a fever, Dr Bruno fanatically so. Sceptical about its use, Byron resisted them as a long as he was able, but, with his system already weakened by the strong purgatives they had administered, he finally gave way and had pints of blood taken from him. When his life ended on 19 April 1824, he could be imagined as having said with Matthew Prior, one of the early English satirists he admired, 'Cur'd yesterday of my Disease/ I died last night of my Physicians.'

Byron's death offers several illustrations of how little power beyond the grave the dead can sometimes have. When he was in Italy, he had made fun of the fact that all the aristocratic patients Polidori managed to acquire after he left his own service had died, and that one of them had been shipped back to England in bits. He was anxious that this should not happen to him, but the Greeks insisted on keeping his lungs. The rest of his corpse was embalmed for transport by sea, but in a way that meant, when there was a brief private exposition of it in London, many of those former friends who came to see him for the last time could barely recognize what

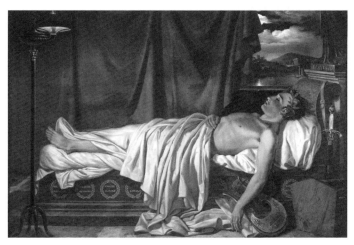

Joseph Odevaere, *Lord Byron on His Deathbed*, c. 1826, oil on canvas.

Memorial tablet in Hucknall parish church.

they saw. He had also asked to be buried in a simple, unostentatious fashion in Missolonghi, but after Hobhouse (at the prompting of Murray) had made an unsuccessful approach to Westminster Abbey, his remains were laid to rest in the parish church closest to Newstead Abbey. His death was front-page news, especially in Europe where he was increasingly celebrated as someone who had given his life so that Greece could become independent. By the time that aim was finally achieved in 1829, he was firmly established as a Greek national hero. Insofar as his ambition had always been to become well known for something other than his writings, this could be considered a satisfactory outcome.

In his own country, however, it is above all as a great writer and the author of at least one major masterpiece in *Don Juan* that Byron most needed, and still needs, to be remembered. Increasingly telling against this outcome has been a tendency that he himself recognized and, in some sense, encouraged. One of Byron's more admirable character traits was his lack of envy. He delighted in Walter Scott's company, considered him the leading writer of

Recent statue of Byron in the grounds of Newstead Abbey.

his generation and read and re-read the Waverley novels with enthusiasm. Yet it was Scott who did more than anyone to turn the general public away from stories in verse to those in prose. Byron himself, of course, often wrote excellent prose and occasionally considered becoming a novelist but had such a wonderful facility with rhyming verse that he was loathe to give it up. The prose he did leave is nonetheless valuable and often of excellent quality (in his letters particularly). This makes it all the more lamentable that when Murray began to consider what to do with that memoir of Byron's earlier life, which he had now bought from Moore, he was persuaded by both Hobhouse and those acting on behalf of Lady Byron (none of whom had read it) that it would be best for all concerned if the manuscript was burnt then and there in Murray's grate. After handing over his memoir to Moore, Byron had generously encouraged him to get what he could from Murray for its eventual, post-mortem publication and use the money to alleviate the financial problems from which he knew his friend was at that time suffering. That Moore insisted on paying back the 2,000 guineas Murray had given him for the manuscript, now destroyed, does not make his weak acquiescence in such a major literary crime more forgivable. The destruction of the memoir was yet one more instance of how little the wishes of the dead can sometimes count once they are no longer present to enforce them.

References

Prefatory Note

1 *The Guardian*, 24 January 2010. The poem is, of course, *Don Juan*.

1 Early Days

1 See Thomas Moore, *Life of Lord Byron* (London, 1851), p. 13. Moore says he takes this story from Byron's own memoir of his early life.
2 See Leslie A. Marchand, *Byron: A Biography* (London, 1957), vol. I, p. 78, but the source is again Moore, *Life of Lord Byron*.
3 See Fiona MacCarthy, *Byron: Life and Legend* (London, 2002).
4 C. J. Tyerman, 'Byron's Harrow', *Byron Journal*, XVII/1 (1989), pp. 17–39.
5 Moore, *Life of Lord Byron*, pp. 46–7.
6 Willis W. Pratt, *Byron at Southwell* (Austin, TX, 1948), p. 12.

2 First Publications

1 Brougham's review is reprinted in Andrew Rutherford, ed., *Lord Byron: The Critical Heritage* (London, 1970), pp. 27–32.
2 Leslie A. Marchand, *Byron: A Biography* (London, 1957), pp. 173–4.
3 Phyllis Grosskurth, *Byron: The Flawed Angel* (London, 1997), p. 75.

4 Fame

1 Malcolm Elwin, *Lord Byron's Wife* (London, 1962), p. 152.
2 Ibid., p. 109. Emphasis added.
3 Ibid., p. 166.
4 Peter Gunn, *My Dearest Augusta* (London, 1968), p. 112.

5 Marriage

1 Malcolm Elwin, *Lord Byron's Wife* (London, 1962), p. 217.
2 Leslie A. Marchand, *Byron: A Biography* (London, 1957), vol. II, p. 563.

6 Switzerland

1 See the letter Walter Scott wrote to J.B.S. Morritt in November 1816.
2 In a letter to the *Times Literary Supplement* of 11 August 1995, Curtis Bennett insisted that Shelley was indeed the father of Claire's baby, born in the autumn of 1816 rather than the January of the following year. According to him, Byron was deliberately misinformed of the birth date so that he would believe the baby his. But this case requires so much elaborate and detailed lying on the part of Shelley, Claire and Mary that it seems far-fetched.
3 Donald Reiman, ed., *Shelley and His Circle*, 10 vols (Cambridge, MA, 1986), vol. VII, p. 28.

7 Venice

1 The review appeared in *The Day and New Times* – see Leslie A. Marchand, *Byron: A Biography* (London, 1957), vol. I, p. 699.
2 Peter Gunn, *My Dearest Augusta* (London, 1968), p. 205.
3 Nicholas A. Joukovsky, ed., *The Letters of Thomas Love Peacock* (London, 2001), vol. I, p. 123.
4 Frederick L. Jones, *Letters of Percy Bysshe Shelley* (London, 1964), vol. II, p. 58.

8 Ravenna Twice Over

1 See Andrew Rutherford, ed., *Lord Byron: The Critical Heritage* (London, 1970), pp. 166–73.

2 Byron's reply to *Blackwood's*, which was never published, can be found in Andrew Nicholson, ed., *Lord Byron: The Complete Miscellaneous Prose* (London, 1991), pp. 88–119.

3 Robert Southey, *A Vision of Judgement* (London, 1821), British Library: Historical Reprint Edition.

4 Goethe's remark, in his conversations with Johann Peter Eckermann, was given currency by Matthew Arnold in his essay on Byron in the second series of his *Essays in Criticism*. For a description of Byron's theological reading, see Christine Kenyon Jones in *Byron in Context*, ed. Clara Tuite (Cambridge, 2020), pp. 101–8, at p. 103.

5 T. S. Eliot, *On Poetry and Poets* (London, 1957), p. 196.

9 Pisa and Genoa

1 Andrew Rutherford, ed., *Lord Byron: The Critical Heritage* (London, 1970), pp. 199–205.

2 E. J. Trelawney, *Records of Shelley, Byron and the Author*, ed. David Wright (London, 1973), p. 99.

3 Rutherford, *Lord Byron*, p. 203.

4 The review appeared in the *Courier* on 26 October 1822 and is quoted by William H. Marshall in his *Byron, Shelley, Hunt, and The Liberal* (Philadelphia, PA, 1960), p. 103.

5 Lady Blessington, *Conversations of Lord Byron*, ed. Ernest J. Lovell (Princeton, NJ, 1969), pp. 80–82.

6 Drummond Bone, 'Childe Harold IV, Don Juan and Beppo', in *The Cambridge Companion to Byron*, ed. Bone (Cambridge, 2004), p. 156.

7 Blessington, *Conversations of Lord Byron*, p. 2.

Select Bibliography

Beaton, Roderick, *Byron's War: Romantic Rebellion, Greek Revolution* (Cambridge, 2013)

Blessington, Lady, *Conversations of Lord Byron*, ed. Ernest J. Lovell (Princeton, NJ, 1969)

Bone, Drummond, ed., *The Cambridge Companion to Byron* (2004)

Brand, Emily, *The Fall of the House of Byron* (London, 2020)

Cameron, Kenneth Neill, et al., eds, *Shelley and His Circle*, 10 vols (Cambridge, MA, 1961–2002)

Cochran, Peter, *Byron in London* (Cambridge, 2008). See also https://petercochran.wordpress.com, where any interested reader can find a positive cornucopia of criticism and useful information on Byron.

Eisler, Benita, *Byron: Child of Passion, Fool of Fame* (London, 1999)

Elwin, Malcolm, *Lord Byron's Wife* (London, 1962)

Gittings, Robert, and Jo Manton, *Claire Clairmont and the Shelleys* (Oxford, 1992)

Grosskurth, Phyllis, *Byron: The Flawed Angel* (London, 1997)

Gunn, Peter, *My Dearest Augusta* (London, 1968)

Hay, Daisy, *Young Romantics: The Shelleys, Byron and Other Tangled Lives* (London, 2010)

Holmes, Richard, *Shelley: The Pursuit* (London, 1994)

Lamb, Lady Caroline, *Glenarvon*, ed. Deborah Lutz (Kansas City, MO, 2007)

Lansdown, Richard, *The Cambridge Introduction to Byron* (Cambridge, 2012)

Lovell, Edward J., ed., *His Very Self and Voice: Collected Conversations of Lord Byron* (New York, 1954)

MacCarthy, Fiona, *Byron: Life and Legend* (London, 2002)

McDayter, Ghislaine, *Byromania and the Birth of Celebrity Culture* (Albany, NY, 2009)

McGann, Jerome K., *'Don Juan' in Context* (London, 1976)

—, ed., *The Complete Poetical Works*, 7 vols (Oxford, 1980–93)

—, ed., *Lord Byron: The Major Works* (Oxford, 2008)

Marchand, Leslie A., *Byron: A Biography*, 3 vols (London, 1957)

—, ed., *Byrons Letters and Journals*, 11 vols (1974–94)

Medwin, Thomas, *Conversations of Lord Byron* (Princeton, NJ, 1966)

Milbanke, Ralph (Earl of Lovelace), *Astarte: A Fragment of Truth Concerning Lord Byron* (London, 1921)

Moore, Doris Langley, *Lord Byron: Accounts Rendered* (London, 1974)

—, *The Late Lord Byron* (London, 1976)

Moore, Thomas, *Life and Letters of Lord Byron* (first published by John Murray in 1830 and then in a one-volume edition by Chatto and Windus in 1875)

Pratt, Willis W., *Byron at Southwell* (Austin, TX, 1948)

Rawes, Alan, and Diego Salia, eds, *Byron and Italy* (Manchester, 2017)

Rutherford, Andrew, ed., *Byron: The Critical Heritage* (London, 1970)

Soderholm, James, ed., *Byron and Romanticism* (Cambridge, 2002)

Stocking, Marion K., *The Clairmont Correspondence: Letters of Claire Clairmont, Charles Clairmont and Fanny Imlay Godwin* (Baltimore, MD, 1995)

Trelawney, E. J., *Records of Shelley, Byron and the Author*, ed. David Wright (London, 1973)

Tuite, Clara, *Lord Byron and Scandalous Celebrity* (Cambridge, 2015)

—, ed., *Byron in Context* (Cambridge, 2020)

Major Works

Hours of Idleness (1807)
English Bards and Scotch Reviewers (1809)
Childe Harold's Pilgrimage, Cantos I and II (1812)
The Giaour (1813)
The Bridge of Abydos (1813)
The Corsair (1814)
Lara (1814)
Hebrew Melodies (1815)
The Siege of Corinth and *Parisina* (1816)
Childe Harold's Pilgrimage, Canto III (1816)
The Prisoner of Chillon (1816)
Manfred (1817)
Beppo (1818)
Childe Harold's Pilgrimage, Canto IV (1818)
Mazeppa (1819)
Don Juan, Cantos I and II (1819)
Don Juan, Cantos III, IV and V (1820)
Marino Faliere (1821)
The Two Forscari (1821)
Sardanapalus (1821)
Werner (1822)
The Vision of Judgement (1822)
Heaven and Earth (1823)
The Age of Bronze (1823)
The Island (1823)
Don Juan, Cantos VI, VII and VIII (1823)
Don Juan, Cantos IX, X and XI (1823)
Don Juan, Cantos XII, XIII and XIV (1823)
Don Juan, Cantos XV and XVI (1824)
Hints from Horace (1831)

Photo Acknowledgements

The author and publishers wish to express their thanks to the below sources of illustrative material and/or permission to reproduce it. Some locations of artworks are also given below, in the interest of brevity:

Alamy: pp. 32 (Art Collection), 173 (Heritage Image Partnership Ltd); © Sebastian Ballard 2022: p. 47; Birmingham Museums: p. 107; Bridgeman Images: p. 64; British Museum, London: pp. 15, 28, 50, 88, 153; David Ellis: pp. 16, 23, 97, 102, 119, 128, 177, 178; Government Art Collection, London: p. 68; Groeningemseum, Bruges: p. 176; Harry Ransom Center, University of Texas at Austin: p. 21; John Murray: p. 122; Musée du Louvre, Paris: p. 141; National Galleries of Scotland, Edinburgh: p. 129; National Portrait Gallery, London: pp. 78, 98, 131, 143; Newstead Abbey, Nottinghamshire: pp. 8, 91; Nottingham City Museums and Galleries: p. 10; from Rowland E. Prothero, ed., *The Works of Lord Byron: Letters and Journals*, vol. v (London, 1904), photo University of California Libraries: p. 151; Rijksmuseum, Amsterdam: p. 114; Shutterstock: p. 52 (Giannis Papanikos).